Budgeting

A Guide to Budgeting and Financial Planning

(Master Budgeting and Achieve Financial Freedom With Minimalism)

James Pacheco

Published By **John Kembrey**

James Pacheco

Budgeting: A Guide to Budgeting and Financial Planning (Master Budgeting and Achieve Financial Freedom With Minimalism)

ISBN   978-1-7771142-6-8

Legal & Disclaimer

Table Of Contents

Chapter 1: Debt Repayment Budgeting

Understanding the Importance of Budgeting

Budgeting is a vital capability that each massive own family with jobs and big payments must preserve near. It is the key to engaging in monetary stability and making the most of your difficult-earned cash. In this subchapter, we're able to delve into the importance of budgeting and the manner it could in reality effect numerous regions of your existence, along with personal, own family, journey, marriage ceremony, retirement, and debt reimbursement budgeting.

Personal Budgeting:

Creating and sticking to a personal fee range allows you to take control of your finances. By know-how your income and prices, you can make informed selections approximately a manner to allocate your money. This allows you to prioritize your desires, store for the destiny, and avoid pointless debt.

Family Budgeting:

For massive households with jobs and massive payments, budgeting is crucial for handling ordinary fees and planning for prolonged-term dreams. It allows you track and manage your spending, ensuring that everybody's desires are met on the equal time as however having room for monetary financial savings and emergencies.

Travel Budgeting:

Budgeting for journey lets in you to experience memorable vacations with out breaking the bank. By putting aside a selected amount every month, you may store up for your dream places and explore the arena on the equal time as staying interior your approach.

Wedding Budgeting:

Planning a marriage may be an luxurious enterprise, however with a nicely-notion-out price range, you may have the wedding of your dreams without going into debt.

Budgeting for each issue, collectively with venue, catering, and apparel, guarantees that you stay on route and avoid overspending.

Retirement Budgeting:

Preparing for retirement is important, specifically for large households with jobs and huge payments. Budgeting for retirement lets in you to keep and make investments as it should be, making sure financial protection sooner or later of your golden years. By information your cutting-edge-day fees and projected desires, you may make informed selections approximately your retirement monetary monetary savings and investments.

Debt Repayment Budgeting:

One of the maximum crucial components of budgeting for large households with jobs and big bills is debt reimbursement. By allocating part of your finances to paying off debts systematically, you may unfastened yourself from monetary burdens and work in the path of a debt-free future.

In quit, expertise the significance of budgeting is essential for massive households with jobs and massive payments. Whether it is non-public, family, journey, wedding ceremony, retirement, or debt reimbursement budgeting, budgeting allows you take manipulate of your fee variety, benefit your desires, and strong a strong economic future for your self and your own family. Start these days and acquire the advantages of budgeting!

Overview of Debt Repayment Strategies

In trendy rapid-paced and luxurious international, many big households with jobs locate themselves drowning in a sea of payments and debt. It may be overwhelming and traumatic, however worry now not! This subchapter, titled "Overview of Debt Repayment Strategies," hobbies to offer you with valuable insights and effective techniques to cope with your debt and regain manage over your fee variety.

Budgeting is the cornerstone of any a success debt reimbursement method. By growing a entire non-public price variety, you could choose out out regions in which you could reduce lower decrease returned on charges and allocate more charge range closer to paying off your money owed. This subchapter will delve into the intricacies of budgeting, offering realistic hints and strategies specially tailored to big families with two jobs and big bills.

Furthermore, we will explore specific styles of budgeting which might be relevant on your unique instances. Whether you are looking to devise a family excursion, save for a marriage, or put together for retirement, statistics the nuances of budgeting within the ones niche areas is important for prolonged-term economic stability. We will provide you with the tools and statistics to create powerful travel budgets, marriage ceremony budgets, and retirement budgets, ensuring that you may enjoy these milestones with out compromising your monetary fitness.

However, the primary attention of this subchapter is debt repayment budgeting. We will dissect numerous debt reimbursement techniques, collectively with the snowball method and the avalanche technique, explaining their professionals and cons and supporting making a decision which technique is pleasant suitable in your goals. Additionally, we're able to introduce you to debt consolidation and negotiation strategies, empowering you to take manipulate of your debt and doubtlessly lessen hobby charges and month-to-month bills.

Throughout this subchapter, we can also emphasize the significance of keeping a excellent thoughts-set and staying induced at some stage in your debt reimbursement adventure. We recognize that it can be hard, but with willpower and area, you may advantage economic freedom.

Chapter 2: Creating A Personal Budget

Assessing Income and Expenses

In the arena we stay in in recent times, coping with fee range has come to be greater important than ever, mainly for massive households with jobs and huge bills. It may be a daunting task to hold song of all of the income and fees that include a hectic household. However, with the right strategies and a strong budgeting plan, you can take manage of your monetary state of affairs and pave the way in the course of a debt-unfastened future.

Assessing your income and charges is the primary vital step on this adventure. Understanding wherein your money is coming from and wherein it's far going will provide you with treasured insights into your financial fitness. To start, acquire all of the important files, collectively with pay stubs, economic employer statements, and bills. This will come up with a clean photo of your earnings property and month-to-month fees.

Start through way of calculating your wellknown monthly profits. This includes all resources of earnings, together with salaries, bonuses, and any more profits streams. Once you've got were given the general earnings determine, deduct your steady costs. These are the vital payments which you want to pay each month, together with lease or mortgage payments, utilities, coverage, and loan repayments. Subtracting those constant prices from your profits will offer you with a better idea of methods plenty disposable earnings you have got left.

Next, take a look at your variable expenses. These are the prices that adjust from month to month, consisting of groceries, ingesting out, leisure, and transportation. It is vital to track the ones prices carefully, as they can quick upload up and impact your tremendous rate range. Consider the usage of budgeting apps or spreadsheets to help you categorize and show your variable costs successfully.

Once you've got were given a clear know-how of your profits and expenses, it is time to make changes and prioritize your economic dreams. Identify areas wherein you could reduce over again on spending, which incorporates lowering consuming out or amusement expenses. Allocate a portion of your profits within the route of an emergency fund and monetary financial savings to make sure you have a safety internet for unexpected expenses.

Remember, the essential problem to a hit budgeting is normal tracking and reviewing. Make it a dependancy to evaluate your income and costs on a month-to-month basis and make crucial changes as desired. This will help you stay on the right song within the path of reaching your economic dreams and ultimately becoming debt-unfastened.

In conclusion, assessing profits and expenses is a important element of effective budgeting. By data your financial situation, you can make informed options, prioritize your spending, and paintings in the direction of a debt-loose future. With power of will and subject, big households with jobs and huge payments can attain monetary balance and enjoy a brighter financial destiny.

Setting Financial Goals

In order to gather financial balance and conquer the stressful situations of dealing with large payments on jobs, it's far crucial for huge families to set smooth and manageable monetary desires. This subchapter will guide you via the way of setting financial dreams, providing you with practical strategies to make certain your own family's lengthy-time period financial well-being.

Budgeting lies at the coronary heart of putting and engaging in financial dreams. By developing a complete rate range, you may gain a smooth information of your profits, charges, and functionality financial financial financial savings. Personal budgeting is critical because it permits you to prioritize your spending, ensuring that your difficult-earned cash is allocated inside the course of the most essential components of your existence.

Family budgeting is specifically critical for big families with jobs and large bills. By regarding all circle of relatives participants within the budgeting method, you can foster a feel of teamwork and obligation, in the long run main to higher financial results. This subchapter will provide you with realistic guidelines and equipment to have interaction your family within the budgeting method, making sure anybody is on board and dedicated to challenge your financial goals.

In addition to each day fees, it's far critical to don't forget specific budgeting niches to cope with your specific financial worrying conditions. Travel budgeting will assist you suggest and keep for those lots-wished own family vacations, making sure you may create lasting recollections without straining your budget. Wedding budgeting will guide you thru the technique of making plans a lovely and extremely good wedding ceremony on the same time as staying inside your manner.

Retirement budgeting is each different critical hassle to remember. By placing aside budget for your retirement, you may make certain economic safety and independence on your golden years. This subchapter will offer you with techniques to maximize your retirement monetary economic financial savings, together with pointers on making an investment and taking advantage of employer-sponsored retirement plans.

Lastly, debt compensation budgeting is a vital issue of attaining monetary balance. This subchapter will guide you thru the technique of making a debt repayment plan, helping you prioritize your money owed and increase a technique to pay them off efficiently. By placing particular dreams for debt compensation, you could frequently get rid of your debts and regain control over your finances.

By putting financial desires, carrying out non-public and family budgeting, and addressing precise budgeting niches which include tour, weddings, retirement, and debt repayment, large families with jobs and massive payments can gain monetary balance and secure a terrific future for his or her cherished ones. This subchapter will equip you with the important information and device to take manage of your price range, empowering you to make knowledgeable monetary picks and advantage your prolonged-term goals.

Allocating Funds for Debt Repayment

When it entails handling your fee range as a huge circle of relatives with jobs and large payments, one of the most vital elements is allocating fee variety for debt compensation. Debt may be a notable burden, causing strain and hindering your economic desires. However, with strategic budgeting and careful making plans, you may regain manipulate of your rate variety and artwork in the direction of a debt-unfastened future.

Personal Budgeting:

Creating an extensive non-public price variety is the first step in the direction of allocating budget for debt repayment. Start thru using monitoring your earnings and costs, figuring out areas in which you may reduce lower lower lower back on useless spending. By prioritizing debt reimbursement to your finances, you may allocate a selected quantity each month within the path of clearing your debts.

Family Budgeting:

In a huge circle of relatives, it's far important to encompass all and sundry inside the budgeting approach. Sit down along with your partner and kids to speak about your economic goals and the significance of debt compensation. Encourage your circle of relatives people to contribute their thoughts on the way to shop coins and decrease fees. This way, all of us will revel in blanketed and stimulated to paintings in the course of a debt-loose destiny.

Travel Budgeting:

While it can be tempting to plan extravagant vacations, it's far essential to prioritize debt compensation over tour costs. Consider allocating a part of your journey price variety closer to clearing your debts. You can although experience less high priced circle of relatives vacations thru selecting nearby places or seeking out price range-extraordinary journey alternatives.

Wedding Budgeting:

Weddings may be costly, but it is important to avoid going into debt in your unique day. Allocate a specific quantity out of your finances towards wedding charges and make sure which you stick with it. Consider price-saving measures along with DIY decorations or choosing a smaller, greater intimate birthday celebration. By prioritizing debt compensation, you could start your married existence on a financially strong footing.

Retirement Budgeting:

While debt reimbursement can be your priority, it's miles further important to save for retirement. Allocate a part of your rate variety within the direction of retirement fee variety, ensuring which you are building a stable destiny for yourself and your circle of relatives. Consult with a financial advertising and marketing representative to discover retirement investment options that align collectively along with your financial goals.

Debt Repayment Budgeting:

Lastly, create a selected price range category absolutely for debt compensation. By allocating a difficult and rapid quantity each month in the route of clearing your debts, you could frequently lessen your economic duties. Consider using techniques along with the snowball or avalanche method to repay your debts more correctly.

Remember, allocating price variety for debt compensation calls for challenge and willpower. By prioritizing debt reimbursement in your fee range and regarding your own family within the manner, you may accumulate financial freedom and pave the way for a brighter future.

Chapter 3: Family Budgeting For Big Families

Identifying Family Financial Needs

In order to efficiently control your rate range and create a a fulfillment debt reimbursement price range, it is vital to first identify your own family's economic dreams. Whether you belong to a big own family with two jobs and large bills or are in fact searching for to enhance your budgeting skills, data your monetary wishes is step one in the direction of reaching monetary stability and peace of thoughts.

Budgeting performs a vital feature in dealing with your circle of relatives's finances, and it all starts offevolved offevolved with information your earnings and fees. Begin through calculating your everyday month-to-month earnings, which include salaries, wages, and any greater property of earnings. Once you have were given a easy image of the manner lots cash is coming in, it is time to analyze your expenses.

Personal budgeting is the muse of any successful economic plan. Take the time to tune your month-to-month prices and categorize them into vital and non-important gadgets. This will come up with an concept of in which your coins is going and assist you prioritize your spending. Big families with two jobs and huge bills often find out themselves juggling severa financial duties, which includes mortgage payments, utilities, groceries, and childcare prices. By identifying the ones dreams, you can allocate your assets therefore and ensure that your circle of relatives's essential goals are met earlier than thinking about discretionary spending.

Travel budgeting is some other important component to keep in mind whilst figuring out your circle of relatives's economic needs. While vacations and getaways are vital for rest and awesome time, it's far critical to plot and price range for them in advance. By placing aside a selected quantity each month closer to journey expenses, you can keep away from accumulating debt or overspending whilst the time includes embark to your a good buy-deserved family holiday.

Special occasions like weddings moreover require cautious budgeting. Planning a wedding can be high-priced, but through figuring out your economic desires early on and growing a marriage fee range, you can keep away from vain strain and debt. Allocate a part of your month-to-month earnings within the route of wedding ceremony prices and research rate-powerful options to ensure a memorable day without breaking the financial organization.

Retirement budgeting is vital for ensuring economic protection in the course of your golden years. By figuring out your circle of relatives's extended-term monetary goals and putting apart part of your earnings for retirement monetary financial savings, you may assemble a nest egg so one can provide for a cushty retirement.

Lastly, debt repayment budgeting is of immoderate significance for huge households with jobs and large bills. By identifying your exquisite money owed and developing a finances that prioritizes debt reimbursement, you could artwork inside the path of becoming debt-unfastened and achieving monetary freedom.

In give up, figuring out your circle of relatives's economic goals is step one toward powerful budgeting and debt compensation. By information your profits, monitoring expenses, and prioritizing your economic responsibilities, you could create a budget that addresses the unique dreams of your big family with jobs and large bills. Whether it is private, circle of relatives, journey, marriage ceremony, retirement, or debt repayment budgeting, taking manage of your finances will purpose a brighter and extra steady monetary destiny.

Allocating Funds for Basic Expenses

In the sector of budgeting, allocating charge variety for simple expenses is an vital step in the direction of attaining monetary balance.

This subchapter pursuits to manual huge households with jobs and large bills in effectively coping with their finances and ensuring that their easy wishes are met with out compromising their prolonged-term monetary goals.

For families juggling more than one jobs and going thru huge payments, creating a entire finances is paramount. Start thru figuring out your primary charges, which generally consist of rent or mortgage payments, software bills, groceries, transportation expenses, and healthcare expenses. These are the essential pillars that require ordinary hobby and want to be prioritized in your finances.

To allocate finances for fundamental prices, it's far critical to adopt a disciplined approach. Begin with the resource of assessing your standard profits and evaluating it in your constant prices. If your income exceeds your vital expenses, recollect allocating a element closer to economic economic savings or debt compensation. It is smart to installation an emergency fund, which could act as a safety net during sudden conditions.

However, if your profits falls brief of assembly your easy costs, it will become vital to make changes. Look for areas in which you can lessen decrease again on discretionary spending and redirect the ones finances in the direction of critical dreams. This also can include decreasing ingesting out, entertainment fees, or comparing your subscription services. By prioritizing your simple charges, you make sure that your own family's dreams are met in advance than indulging in non-important charges.

In addition to allocating finances for easy charges, it is critical to set realistic dreams and art work in the direction of them step by step. This subchapter caters to numerous niches, on the facet of private budgeting, circle of relatives budgeting, tour budgeting, bridal ceremony budgeting, retirement budgeting, and debt repayment budgeting. Each area of interest calls for tailor-made techniques and issues, but the underlying principle stays the equal – prioritizing crucial charges at the same time as working within the course of financial safety and prolonged-time period dreams.

Remember, budgeting is an ongoing way that requires regular evaluation and modifications. As your circle of relatives's events trade, your monetary priorities also can shift as well. Stay proactive and make the crucial adjustments for your price range to make sure that your essential charges are accurately blanketed.

By efficiently allocating price variety for easy charges, huge households with jobs and massive bills can enjoy financial stability and peace of mind. This subchapter equips them with the crucial equipment and strategies to navigate their particular monetary landscape and obtain their prolonged-time period dreams.

Budgeting for Children's Education and Activities

In modern-day global, raising a own family on the equal time as juggling jobs and dealing with big payments may be a monetary venture. As mother and father, we need the exceptional for our youngsters, together with a best education and the opportunity to participate in numerous sports activities sports. However, the ones prices can short upload up and strain our already tight budgets. That's why it's miles important for huge households with jobs and large bills to have a strong plan in region for budgeting their children's training and sports sports.

Personal Budgeting: The first step in managing your kid's education and sports activities is to create a whole non-public price range. This rate range have to embody all assets of profits, month-to-month fees, and economic financial savings dreams. By prioritizing your kid's education and sports activities within your charge range, you could allocate price range for that reason and ensure their needs are met.

Family Budgeting: As a huge circle of relatives, it's far critical to involve surely everybody in the budgeting approach. Sit down collectively and discuss the monetary goals you've got have been given to your kid's training and activities. Encourage your kids to make contributions to the talk, training them the price of cash and the importance of budgeting from an early age.

Travel Budgeting: Family vacations and trips can be an enriching enjoy for kids, however they can also be luxurious. With cautious making plans and budgeting, you can make the ones trips low value and amusing. Research a lot less highly-priced tour options, set a adventure price range, and incorporate your youngsters inside the choice-making gadget. This manner, they will discover ways to recognize the fee of cash and make responsible alternatives.

Wedding Budgeting: Planning a wedding on your little one may be overwhelming, each emotionally and financially. To avoid going into debt, it's miles essential to set a wedding fee range and stick with it. Encourage your little one to prioritize their wants and needs, and discover innovative procedures to maintain cash without compromising at the party.

Retirement Budgeting: While focusing for your children's education and sports activities, it is crucial not to overlook your personal financial future. Allocate a part of your price range towards retirement financial savings so you can sturdy a comfortable future for your self and your own family.

Debt Repayment Budgeting: Big families often face the task of coping with amazing debts. Prioritize debt compensation interior your charge variety and allocate rate variety closer to paying off excessive-hobby money owed. By being proactive in dealing with your debts, you can loose up extra assets for your children's schooling and sports activities.

In give up, budgeting for children's education and sports activities is critical for big families with jobs and large bills. By creating a complete non-public fee range, regarding the whole circle of relatives, and prioritizing costs, you could make sure that your children get hold of the training and opportunities they deserve on the equal time as staying interior your economic method. Remember, with cautious planning and budgeting, you can offer your youngsters with a satisfying youth without sacrificing your economic balance.

Saving for Emergencies and Future Expenses

In the short-paced worldwide we live in nowadays, unexpected emergencies and destiny charges can rise up at any 2d. As a massive circle of relatives with jobs and massive bills, it's far essential to have a plan in area for the ones conditions to make certain financial balance. This subchapter will manual you through the way of saving for emergencies and future fees, supplying practical techniques that may be completed to various additives of your finances.

Budgeting is the cornerstone of economic fulfillment, and private budgeting is particularly crucial for large families like yours. By cautiously monitoring your earnings and charges, you can find out areas wherein you may lessen lower decrease back and redirect those finances in the route of your emergency economic financial savings. It is usually encouraged to allocate a percent of your month-to-month earnings particularly for emergencies and future fees. Start small, although it is only some greenbacks, and frequently growth the quantity as you become extra cushty with saving.

Family budgeting is every different location of hobby which could notably advantage from a committed emergency fund. Unexpected clinical payments, automobile maintenance, or domestic safety can fast drain your budget if you are unprepared. By placing apart a part of your rate variety for emergencies, you are making sure that your circle of relatives's financial properly-being stays intact at the identical time as the ones unexpected costs arise.

Travel budgeting and wedding ceremony budgeting are also regions in which having an emergency fund is essential. While it's miles interesting to devise a dream tour or a fairy-tale wedding ceremony, it's far similarly crucial to undergo in mind sudden prices which can upward push up. By saving in advance, you can reduce the impact of those more fees and revel in your particular moments with out monetary pressure.

Retirement budgeting is an extended-term motive that need to no longer be omitted. As a large circle of relatives with jobs and large bills, it can appear difficult to buy retirement. However, thru which include retirement savings as a part of your monthly price range, you are ensuring a stable destiny for yourself and your loved ones.

Finally, debt reimbursement budgeting is an crucial factor of monetary balance. By allocating a part of your rate range toward paying off money owed, you can frequently get rid of them and unfastened up more price variety for emergencies and destiny charges.

In conclusion, saving for emergencies and future fees is important for big households with jobs and large payments. By implementing techniques which include private budgeting, own family budgeting, journey budgeting, marriage ceremony budgeting, retirement budgeting, and debt repayment budgeting, you could accumulate financial balance and peace of mind. Start small, be regular, and watch your emergency fund increase, presenting you with a safety internet for something existence throws your manner.

Chapter 4: Travel Budgeting

Planning and Saving for Vacations

When you've got were given a massive family, two jobs, and massive payments to pay, it may seem not possible to plan and preserve for a holiday. However, with careful budgeting and smart economic techniques, you can make your dream excursion a reality. In this subchapter, we're able to explore the importance of making plans and saving for vacations and provide sensible hints to help you acquire your journey desires.

Budgeting is the foundation of any a fulfillment economic plan, and it's far critical as regards to saving for vacations. Start with the aid of growing a whole non-public fee range that consists of all of your income property and expenses, such as payments, groceries, and debt bills. By tracking your spending, you could find out regions in which you may reduce once more and redirect the ones finances inside the direction of your vacation financial financial savings.

Family budgeting is an crucial detail of making plans for holidays, because it consists of the participation of all own family individuals. Sit down together with your partner and youngsters and communicate the importance of saving for holidays. Encourage all people to make a contribution to the vacation fund by using manner of way of decreasing useless fees or taking over greater detail-time jobs. This now not handiest teaches your youngsters the fee of coins however moreover instills a enjoy of ownership and exhilaration for the imminent experience.

Travel budgeting is a niche that focuses specially on saving for vacations. Consider installing place a separate economic monetary financial savings account committed mostly on your adventure desires. Automate regular contributions to this account, whether or no longer or not it's miles weekly, bi-weekly, or monthly, to make certain consistent development in the direction of your holiday fund. Additionally, discover strategies to reduce tour charges, collectively with reserving earlier, the use of travel rewards programs, or deciding on greater much less high-priced locations.

While holidays are a exquisite enjoy, it's far crucial to strike a balance amongst playing the triumphing and saving for the future. Retirement budgeting is a vital detail of monetary planning, and it ought to not be neglected at the equal time as saving for vacations. Allocate a part of your monetary financial savings within the route of retirement bills to make sure lengthy-term financial safety.

Lastly, debt compensation budgeting is vital for big families with jobs and huge payments. Prioritize paying off immoderate-hobby debts, which incorporates credit score gambling playing cards or private loans, earlier than allocating finances in the direction of vacations. By reducing your debt burden, you'll have more financial flexibility to keep for and enjoy your tour with out annoying about mounting hobby fees.

In stop, planning and saving for vacations requires careful budgeting and smart financial techniques. By growing a personal price range, related to your family, putting in region a committed monetary savings account, and balancing your financial priorities, you can make your dream vacation a fact even as staying on pinnacle of your monetary duties. Remember, with strength of will and location, you could advantage your tour dreams and create lasting reminiscences on your massive family.

Finding Affordable Travel Options

When you've got got a huge own family with two jobs and huge bills, it can occasionally sense like a expensive to even bear in mind taking a vacation. However, with cautious planning and budgeting, it's miles feasible to find less expensive tour options which could provide tons-needed relaxation and notable time for your family. In this subchapter, we are able to discover diverse strategies and hints to help you make the most of your journey rate range.

1. Plan in Advance: One of the keys to finding low-cost journey alternatives is to plan your trips properly earlier. This lets in you to take benefit of early bird discounts, promotional gives, and less luxurious flight tickets. By reserving early, you may additionally solid low cost lodges alternatives and avoid peak season rate hikes.

2. Research Budget Destinations: Not all excursion places have to interrupt the financial organization. Look for price range-excellent alternatives that provide a range of sights and sports activities sports suitable to your family. Consider locations with lower prices of dwelling or places which are less popular but though offer unique studies.

three. Flexible Travel Dates: Being flexible collectively together with your excursion dates will allow you to keep appreciably on transportation and inns. Avoid travelling during top seasons or weekends even as expenses are commonly better. Instead, choose mid-week or off-top tour, which frequently comes with decreased prices.

four. Consider Alternative Accommodation: Instead of traditional lodges, discover possibility accommodations options which encompass vacation rentals, hostels, or perhaps residence swaps. These alternatives can often offer more place to your circle of relatives at a fraction of the charge.

5. Take Advantage of Travel Rewards: If you have got got were given credit rating gambling playing playing cards or loyalty programs, make sure to take gain of the adventure rewards they provide. Accumulate elements or miles with the beneficial resource of the use of your gambling playing cards for normal fees and redeem them for discounted flights, inn remains, or possibly free enhancements.

6. Pack Smart and Save: Another way to store coins on journey is thru the usage of packing smart. Avoid overpacking and paying extra

luggage costs. Research airline bags policies and % moderate to avoid additional charges. Additionally, don't forget bringing your non-public snacks and drinks for the journey to keep away from costly airport expenses.

Remember, low-cost journey options are possible even for large households with jobs and huge payments. By enforcing those strategies and pointers, you may create unforgettable memories with out setting a pressure to your charge variety. With careful making plans and a piece creativity, you could enjoy quality time together with your circle of relatives while preserving your economic dreams intact.

Budgeting for Transportation, Accommodation, and Activities

Transportation, lodges, and sports sports are high-quality charges which can quick eat away at your rate variety if not well managed. As a massive circle of relatives with jobs and large payments, it's miles critical to be careful approximately the manner you allocate your charge variety in the direction of these areas. In this subchapter, we're able to discuss powerful techniques for budgeting in phrases of transportation, accommodations, and sports activities.

Transportation fees can be a number one drain in your budget, specifically if you have a huge own family. One manner to preserve cash on transportation is by means of the usage of the use of public transportation each time feasible. Research close by bus or teach routes and don't forget purchasing month-to-month passes, as they regularly provide big financial savings in evaluation to man or woman tickets. Carpooling is each other remarkable desire, permitting you to percentage the prices of fuel and automobile maintenance with others.

When it entails accommodation, maintain in thoughts alternatives to pricey accommodations. Look for finances-excellent options alongside side holiday leases, hostels, or maybe tenting if suitable to your own family. Websites like Airbnb and VRBO assist you to discover much less high priced and snug lodges that meet your goals. Additionally, bear in mind journeying at some stage in off-top seasons at the same time as expenses will be predisposed to be lower.

Activities can brief add up, specially for a massive own family. To stay inner your budget, plan ahead and research unfastened or low-value sports inside the region you are touring. Look for close by parks, museums with discounted or loose admission days, or community activities that offer entertainment without breaking the economic organization. Take gain of any discounts to be had for families or massive agencies, together with institution expenses for excursions or attractions.

In addition to transportation, inns, and sports activities, it is vital to allocate a portion of your finances to sudden costs which can arise in the course of your experience. Setting aside a small emergency fund will offer you with peace of mind and prevent you from going into debt if some issue sudden takes vicinity.

Remember, budgeting for transportation, accommodation, and sports calls for cautious planning and research. By being proactive and making informed selections, you can revel in memorable tales without sacrificing your economic balance.

Chapter 5: Wedding Budgeting

Setting a Realistic Wedding Budget

Planning a wedding can be an exciting time for any couple, however for massive families with jobs and huge payments, it may additionally be a monetary challenge. However, with cautious budgeting and strategic planning, it's miles feasible to have a cute wedding ceremony without breaking the economic group. In this financial disaster, we're capable of find out a way to set a practical wedding ceremony budget that fits the needs and economic competencies of massive households.

Budgeting is a essential trouble of any a hit financial plan, and weddings are not any exception. To start, it's miles vital to assess your modern-day monetary situation. Take into consideration your earnings, charges, and any present debt or economic commitments. Understanding your economic repute will assist you decide how a good deal you could realistically allocate closer to your wedding ceremony finances.

Next, keep in mind your priorities as a pair. What factors of the marriage are maximum essential to you? Is it the venue, catering, pictures, or the overall atmosphere? By identifying your priorities, you could allocate a larger a part of your budget to those key areas while being more frugal in less vital factors.

Research is essential close to setting a sensible wedding ceremony charge variety. Gather statistics approximately the not unusual prices of numerous marriage ceremony factors to your location. This will give you a better know-how of what to expect and assist you to make informed selections.

Creating an in depth price range spreadsheet is an powerful manner to maintain tune of your fees. List all of the crucial marriage ceremony factors together with venue, catering, attire, decorations, pix, and transportation, on the aspect in their expected costs. Be high quality to head away some room for unexpected costs or emergencies.

Consider opportunity alternatives that let you shop cash without compromising on notable. For example, in vicinity of reserving an steeply-priced venue, you could find out more reasonably-priced alternatives which encompass community halls or out of doors areas. Similarly, hiring a professional but lesser-diagnosed photographer may be a cost-effective opportunity to an high priced professional.

Lastly, be open and sincere together with your family and friends approximately your finances boundaries. They will understand and respect your economic barriers. In truth, they will actually have creative ideas or connections that permit you to shop cash.

Setting a sensible wedding ceremony finances is important for huge families with jobs and large bills. By carefully making plans, getting to know, and prioritizing, you can have a memorable bridal ceremony that suits inside your monetary way. Remember, it isn't about how a superb deal you spend however the love and delight you proportion for your precise day.

Prioritizing Wedding Expenses

Planning a wedding may be an thrilling enjoy, but it could moreover be financially overwhelming, specifically for big families with jobs and large payments. However, with right budgeting strategies, you can make certain that your dream wedding ceremony might not come to be a burden for your fee range. In this subchapter, we're able to discuss the significance of prioritizing bridal ceremony charges and offer you with guidelines to create a finances that fits your monetary state of affairs.

When it includes bridal ceremony planning, it's miles crucial to set up your priorities right from the begin. Sit down together with your partner and speak what additives of the marriage are most important to both of you.

Is it the venue, the food, the decorations, or the apparel? By identifying your priorities, you may allocate your finances for that reason and keep away from overspending on much less widespread factors.

Personal budgeting performs a critical characteristic in handling marriage ceremony fees. Create a separate budget in your bridal ceremony and determine how a first rate deal you may realistically manage to pay for to spend. Consider your modern monetary responsibilities, which consist of payments, loans, and savings dreams, and allocate a part of your earnings within the path of the wedding fund. This will help you prevent useless debt and make certain a smoother transition into married lifestyles.

Family budgeting is any other crucial element to take into account. If you have a massive own family, it's miles possibly that they may need to make contributions to the marriage prices. Be open and obvious together with your family approximately your economic state of affairs and allow them to apprehend how they're able to assist. This can consist of financial contributions, DIY duties, or perhaps lending their talents and talents for numerous wedding ceremony responsibilities.

Travel budgeting is regularly not noted on the identical time as making plans a wedding. If your own family and buddies are scattered in the course of one-of-a-kind locations, journey fees can fast add up. Consider possibility alternatives which incorporates destination weddings or choosing a venue that is with out trouble accessible for most visitors. Additionally, search for tour gives, organization reductions, or undergo in mind carpooling to keep on transportation fees.

Lastly, do not forget that your wedding ceremony is without a doubt at some point in your lifetime together. While it is essential to have a top notch time this precise event, it's similarly essential to plan for your destiny. Retirement budgeting and debt reimbursement should now not be not noted subsequently of the wedding making plans approach. Allocate a part of your price variety closer to retirement savings and hold making normal debt payments to stay on the right song toward your economic dreams.

In cease, prioritizing wedding ceremony fees is critical for massive households with jobs and large payments. By putting in your priorities, growing a separate wedding ceremony price variety, concerning your circle of relatives, considering adventure charges, and retaining an eye constant steady for your long-term monetary desires, you may have a memorable wedding without breaking the economic company. Remember, it's far not the grandeur of the event but the love and commitment shared that sincerely depend.

Cutting Costs without Sacrificing Quality

In extremely-contemporary fast-paced international, many big families with jobs and massive payments locate it tough to manipulate their price range efficaciously. Budgeting turns into an important device for these households to live on pinnacle in their costs and debt reimbursement. However, often, the concept of decreasing costs can evoke a enjoy of sacrifice and compromise on first rate. But be involved not! This subchapter is here to manual you on how to reduce prices without compromising on the subjects that undergo in thoughts most.

When it includes budgeting, the secret is to come to be aware about areas in which you may make big financial savings without sacrificing first-rate. One of the only strategies to collect that is with the useful useful resource of evaluating your spending behavior and making considerate picks. Start through the usage of manner of tracking your charges meticulously to find out any unnecessary or impulse purchases. This will provide you with a clean understanding of wherein your coins go and assist you prioritize your spending.

Another method to lessen costs without sacrificing quality is thru manner of locating options in your cutting-edge-day fees. For instance, in case you're spending a huge part of your price range on eating out, do not forget cooking at domestic more often. This not most effective saves coins however also permits you to control the wonderful and dietary value of your meals. Similarly, as an alternative of buying high priced branded merchandise, find out commonplace or shop producers that provide extraordinary excellent at a lower price.

Big households frequently face first rate charges with reference to adventure, weddings, and retirement planning. However, with cautious making plans and budgeting, those prices may be managed efficiently. When it includes excursion, recollect reserving flights and resorts at some point of off-pinnacle seasons or taking advantage of final-minute offers. Wedding budgeting may be difficult, however through the usage of prioritizing the maximum crucial elements and being innovative with decorations and favors, you can have a memorable party without breaking the monetary organization. And for retirement budgeting, undergo in mind working with monetary advisors who deliver attention to helping households with jobs and big bills to ensure you're making the maximum of your investments.

Remember, cutting fees does no longer suggest sacrificing splendid; it manner being aware about your spending and making options that align collectively along with your economic desires. By imposing those techniques, massive households with two jobs and massive payments can efficiently manage their price range, reduce debt, and create a extra everyday destiny.

Managing Post-Wedding Finances

After the joyous party of your wedding ceremony day, it's critical to shift your cognizance to dealing with your submit-bridal ceremony price range. As a huge own family with jobs and massive bills, it's miles critical to create a solid plan to ensure that you can hold monetary stability and obtain your lengthy-term dreams. In this subchapter, we are able to talk powerful techniques for coping with your put up-wedding ceremony finances.

First and fundamental, it's far crucial to create a entire budget that considers all additives of your economic life. Personal budgeting is a key expertise that will help you track your fees, set monetary goals, and allocate your earnings effectively. Take the time to sit down down down together with your associate and examine your cutting-edge economic situation. Consider your monthly income, bills, and any fantastic money owed. By know-how your financial responsibilities, you could make informed picks concerning your spending behavior and economic savings functionality.

Family budgeting is some other important element to take into account. As a huge circle of relatives, it is vital to incorporate all individuals in the budgeting device. Encourage open conversation approximately financial dreams and priorities. This will now not handiest instill a enjoy of duty for your kids but also can even help you are making collective selections that gain the complete own family.

While budgeting, it's far vital to allocate budget for tour. As a huge circle of relatives, vacations may be a project, however with proper making plans and budgeting, you may despite the fact that create memorable research without breaking the financial group. Set apart a journey budget that cash owed for transportation, accommodations, food, and amusement. Consider possibility options collectively with road journeys or camping, which can be greater fee-effective even as even though providing an thrilling enjoy for the whole circle of relatives.

Additionally, it's miles essential to address any marriage ceremony-related debts and prioritize debt compensation budgeting. Weddings may be costly, and it's miles not unusual to incur a few debt at some point of this time. Create a plan to cope with those money owed systematically, specializing in excessive-hobby money owed first. Consider consolidating your debts or negotiating lower hobby expenses to make the reimbursement way extra possible.

Lastly, recall about retirement budgeting. As a huge family with jobs and massive payments, it is simple to overlook saving for retirement. However, it's miles important to start planning on your future early on. Allocate part of your income within the route of retirement monetary financial financial savings, whether or not or no longer thru organization-backed plans or man or woman retirement bills (IRAs). Consult a economic consultant if critical to make sure that you are maximizing your retirement economic financial savings functionality.

Chapter 6: Retirement Budgeting

Understanding Retirement Savings and Investments

Retirement is a segment of existence that all of us aspire to revel in. It is the time whilst we're able to ultimately lighten up, tour the arena, and spend exceptional time with our loved ones. However, to be able to have a snug and worry-unfastened retirement, it is vital to start saving and making an funding early on. This subchapter targets to help large families with jobs and massive bills apprehend the importance of retirement economic financial savings and investments and gives valuable strategies to ensure a stable financial future.

Budgeting plays a vital function in retirement planning. By growing a personal price variety, you could understand areas wherein you may lessen down expenses and allocate more toward retirement financial savings. This subchapter delves into the only-of-a-type sorts of budgets, which include non-public budgeting, circle of relatives budgeting, excursion budgeting, wedding ceremony budgeting, and retirement budgeting, presenting practical recommendations and techniques to control budget effectively.

When it entails retirement monetary monetary savings, it's far crucial to start early and take benefit of compound interest. This subchapter explains the electricity of compound interest and demonstrates how even small contributions made constantly over time can cause incredible growth in retirement price range. It moreover discusses various retirement financial savings alternatives which consist of business corporation-subsidized retirement plans like 401(k) and person retirement bills (IRAs), highlighting their benefits and tax advantages.

Investing is some other key element of retirement planning. This subchapter affords a top stage view of diverse investment vehicles together with shares, bonds, mutual charge variety, and actual assets. It explains a way to determine danger tolerance and pick investments that align with lengthy-time period economic dreams. It discusses the idea of diversification and emphasizes the importance of frequently reviewing and rebalancing investment portfolios to make sure first-class returns.

Furthermore, the subchapter explores the idea of debt repayment budgeting. It gives strategies for coping with debt efficaciously, in conjunction with prioritizing immoderate-hobby debts, negotiating lower interest charges, and developing a debt repayment plan. By lowering debt burdens, humans and families can loose up extra price range to shop for retirement.

Overall, "Understanding Retirement Savings and Investments" is an entire subchapter that equips large families with the statistics and system they want to plan for a stable and comfortable retirement. By imposing the techniques stated on this subchapter, readers can take manipulate in their price variety, benefit their retirement goals, and revel in a worry-unfastened destiny.

Estimating Retirement Expenses

Retirement is a time of existence that many individuals and households appearance earlier to. It's a time to lighten up, enjoy the quit end result of your hard paintings, and spend first rate time with cherished ones. However, on the manner to really enjoy your retirement years, it's far important to plot ahead and estimate your retirement prices efficaciously. This bankruptcy will manual big families with jobs and huge bills through the system of estimating retirement prices, ensuring a financially stable and strain-free retirement.

One of the primary steps in estimating retirement fees is to evaluate your present day-day lifestyle and decide how it could change during retirement. Consider factors which include housing fees, transportation charges, healthcare needs, and entertainment sports. For massive families with jobs and large bills, it's far crucial to account for the functionality boom in healthcare charges, in addition to the opportunity of assisting adult kids or developing vintage dad and mom.

Next, it is important to consider any expected assets of retirement income. This might also encompass pensions, social protection blessings, investment earnings, and every distinct assets of passive earnings. By facts your anticipated earnings, you can because it must be estimate how masses you could want to cowl any gaps and preserve your desired favored of living finally of retirement.

Once you have a easy data of your expected earnings and expected charges, it's time to create a retirement price range. A retirement price range will assist you allocate your property correctly and make knowledgeable choices approximately saving, spending, and making an funding. It is generally endorsed to talk over with a financial consultant specializing in retirement planning to make sure your price range aligns together collectively together with your lengthy-time period goals.

Additionally, it is essential to often assessment and alter your retirement finances as situations trade. Life is unpredictable, and unexpected charges or modifications in income can impact your retirement plans. By often comparing your rate range, you could make critical changes and make certain your monetary protection in retirement.

In end, estimating retirement prices is a vital element of financial planning for big households with jobs and huge bills. By cautiously thinking about your way of life, income resources, and expected fees, you could create a practical retirement price variety if you want to provide peace of mind and allow you to experience your golden years to the fullest. Remember to regularly evaluation and alter your finances as had to adapt to converting instances and keep a financially solid retirement.

Creating a Retirement Budget

As a member of a massive own family with two jobs and massive payments, planning for retirement can also moreover appear like a daunting task. However, with right budgeting and financial subject, you may make certain a comfortable and strain-loose retirement. This subchapter will manual you thru the crucial steps of creating a retirement rate range that suits your specific scenario.

Personal budgeting is the muse of any a hit monetary plan, together with retirement planning. Begin through assessing your contemporary-day profits and expenses. Calculate how plenty you can hold each month and set apart a detail for retirement. Remember, the sooner you start saving, the extra time your money has to broaden via investments.

Family budgeting is critical while planning for retirement. Involve your companion and kids in the approach so that everybody is privy to the economic goals and can contribute to saving for retirement. Discuss the importance of reducing useless costs and locating strategies to increase earnings to maximise economic savings.

Travel budgeting and wedding budgeting can also moreover seem unrelated to retirement making plans, but they're massive prices that could effect your ability to shop. By developing a separate fee range for the ones occasions, you can ensure that they do now not prevent your retirement economic savings. Look for fee-effective methods to devise a memorable wedding ceremony and prioritize journey charges primarily based definitely on your retirement dreams.

Retirement budgeting calls for cautious attention of different factors. Estimate your positioned up-retirement prices, taking into consideration healthcare charges, housing, every day dwelling costs, and each special financial commitments. Consider consulting a financial representative that will help you determine the proper quantity to keep and the extremely good funding options to build up your retirement desires.

Debt reimbursement budgeting is important to assignment a debt-unfastened retirement. Prioritize paying off excessive-hobby money owed which include credit score gambling cards and loans to unfastened up extra cash for retirement monetary economic savings. Explore debt consolidation alternatives and negotiate with creditors to lessen interest costs or create a more feasible charge plan.

Creating a retirement price range can also require a few sacrifices and manner of lifestyles modifications, but it's far important for securing your economic future. Keep music of your retirement financial savings often and make changes as wished. By sticking in your charge range and making knowledgeable monetary choices, you can revel in a snug retirement and offer for your family's desires.

Remember, it's miles in no way too early or too beyond due to start making plans for retirement. Start in recent times, and take control of your monetary destiny.

Strategies for Catching Up on Retirement Savings

In present day fast-paced global, many big households with jobs and huge payments discover themselves suffering to shop for retirement. Balancing normal charges, debt reimbursement, and the choice to experience life have to make it difficult to set aside coins for the future. However, it's in no way too past because of start catching up on retirement financial savings. In this subchapter, we will talk effective strategies that assist you to solid a snug retirement.

1. Assess your current scenario: Begin with the aid of evaluating your present day monetary recognition. Determine how a great deal you have stored for retirement, estimate your prices in the path of retirement, and calculate the space the diverse 2. This will give you a easy image of the way plenty you need to capture up.

2. Create an extensive rate variety: Budgeting is crucial for any own family, specially those dealing with a couple of incomes and substantial bills. Allocate a part of your earnings closer to retirement financial savings, similar to some other fee. By developing a sensible rate variety, you can find out regions wherein you may lessen decrease lower back and redirect price range towards your retirement desires.

three. Increase your profits: Consider techniques to enhance your earnings, alongside facet taking up extra component-time art work or starting a element business corporation. Every more greenback earned may be positioned in the direction of your retirement financial economic savings, helping you lure up quicker.

4. Cut unnecessary fees: Take a hard have a look at your prices and turn out to be aware of regions wherein you could make cuts. This would in all likelihood embody ingesting out a good deal much less regularly, reducing

entertainment prices, or locating more an awful lot much less high-priced alternatives for regular devices. By being privy to your spending, you can unfastened up additional finances for retirement financial savings.

5. Maximize retirement contributions: Take gain of retirement financial savings plans supplied thru your corporation, which incorporates a 401(good enough) or 403(b). Contribute the most amount allowed, mainly in case your enterprise commercial enterprise corporation gives an identical contribution. Additionally, find out other retirement financial savings options, such as IRAs, and make everyday contributions to maximise your economic financial savings potential.

6. Seek professional recommendation: Consider consulting with a financial advertising and marketing representative who makes a speciality of retirement planning. They will will let you amplify a customized approach based actually to your unique situations. A expert can also manual you on

investment alternatives that can accelerate your retirement economic savings.

Remember, catching up on retirement economic financial savings requires area, staying electricity, and determination. By imposing those strategies and making retirement financial savings a priority, you can take big strides inside the direction of securing a cushty future for yourself and your family. Start these days, and you'll be to your manner to a worry-free retirement.

Chapter 7: Debt Repayment Strategies For Big Families

Assessing Debt and Creating a Repayment Plan

Debt Repayment Budgeting: Strategies for Big Families with Two Jobs and Big Bills

Chapter four: Assessing Debt and Creating a Repayment Plan

Introduction:

In this subchapter, we're able to delve into the essential step of assessing your debt and growing a reimbursement plan. As large households with jobs and massive payments, it's miles crucial to take manage of your monetary situation and growth a way to repay money owed efficaciously. By information the diverse components of debt evaluation and developing a compensation plan, you'll be on your way to accomplishing economic freedom.

Assessing Your Debt:

The first step in tackling your debt is to assess the whole quantity of what you owe. Gather all relevant economic documents, which embody credit score rating card statements, loan agreements, and splendid payments. Create a comprehensive list of your debts, noting the brilliant balances, interest prices, and minimal monthly payments. This will offer you with a clean photograph of your financial obligations.

Prioritizing Debts:

Once you have a complete list of money owed, it's miles important to prioritize them. Identify immoderate-hobby money owed, along with credit score rating playing playing cards or payday loans, as they could quickly acquire interest and grow to be unmanageable. Consider growing a debt snowball or debt avalanche plan, where you both repay the smallest debt first or attention on the most effective with the pleasant interest charge. This will help you live brought on and make improvement toward becoming debt-free.

Creating a Repayment Plan:

With a easy facts of your money owed and prioritization in area, it is time to create a reimbursement plan. Start with the useful useful resource of setting up a realistic charge range that lets in for debt repayment on the equal time as assembly your circle of relatives's crucial dreams. Determine how heaps you may allocate inside the path of debt compensation each month and hold on with it.

Consider negotiating lower hobby charges or exploring debt consolidation alternatives to simplify your repayment plan. Make extraordinary to communicate along side your creditors and lenders to find out solutions that artwork for every events.

Monitoring and Adjusting:

Regularly screen your improvement and make adjustments as wanted. Celebrate small wins alongside the manner to preserve motivation. If you stumble upon unexpected economic setbacks, be bendy and adapt your repayment plan consequently.

Conclusion:

Assessing your debt and growing a reimbursement plan is a critical step towards undertaking monetary balance for big households with jobs and huge payments. By information your money owed, prioritizing them, and growing a realistic reimbursement plan, you can regain control of your fee variety and paintings toward a debt-loose future. Remember, it's by no means too past due to begin, and with willpower and place, you may conquer any financial undertaking.

Prioritizing Debts and Negotiating with Creditors

In the world of large families with two jobs and big payments, managing money owed can regularly enjoy overwhelming. However, with the proper techniques and a targeted method, it's miles viable to regain manipulate over your economic situation. This subchapter will delve into the importance of prioritizing debts and provide steerage on the way to barter with lenders effectively.

One of the primary steps in debt repayment budgeting is to evaluate your extraordinary money owed and prioritize them based on their urgency and effect in your financial well-being. Start through listing all of your debts, along with credit score rating score card balances, loans, and superb payments. Categorize them into vital and non-critical money owed. Essential debts might also consist of loan or lease bills, utilities, and insurance costs, at the same time as non-critical debts may be credit score card debt or personal loans.

Once you have were given identified your debts, it is crucial to allocate your to be had fee variety wisely. Focus on paying off important money owed first to make certain that your fundamental wishes are met and to keep away from any ability results together with eviction or software program application disconnections. Prioritizing critical money owed furthermore enables in keeping a strong basis to your economic future.

Negotiating with lenders is each other crucial problem of debt repayment. Many creditors are inclined to artwork with borrowers who monitor a proactive technique and a real strength of mind to paying off their debts. Start via contacting your lenders and explaining your economic state of affairs. Discuss the opportunity of negotiating reduced hobby costs, lower monthly bills, or extended repayment phrases. It is crucial to have a easy know-how of your fee range and what type of you may realistically manage to pay for to pay toward each debt.

When negotiating with lenders, be prepared to offer documentation that enables your monetary trouble. This can also encompass pay stubs, monetary business enterprise statements, or scientific bills. Presenting a whole picture of your economic situation can boom your chances of wearing out a advantageous agreement.

Remember, negotiating with lenders requires staying electricity and staying electricity. It may furthermore take severa tries to acquire a suitable affiliation. Stay focused for your cause of debt compensation and live dedicated to the manner.

In stop, prioritizing debts and negotiating with creditors are vital steps in the course of attaining economic balance for big families with jobs and huge payments. By identifying and addressing your maximum urgent debts first and correctly negotiating with lenders, you could regain manage over your economic state of affairs and pave the way for a brighter future.

Strategies for Increasing Income

In ultra-present day fast-paced worldwide, many large households with jobs and large payments find it difficult to make ends meet.

However, thru enforcing powerful strategies for growing profits, it is possible to alleviate economic burdens and advantage financial balance. This subchapter will find out numerous strategies that would assist huge households boom their profits and decorate their financial scenario.

1. Side Hustles: One of the maximum well-known strategies to boom income is thru the use of taking up a thing hustle. This can also want to contain starting a small organisation, freelancing, or imparting offerings which incorporates tutoring, domestic dog sitting, or domestic cleansing. By leveraging capabilities and skills outdoor of regular employment, huge households can generate additional income streams.

2. Monetizing Hobbies: Many individuals have interests that may be modified into worthwhile ventures. Whether it's miles crafting, portray, baking, or gardening, massive households can learn how to monetize their passions and earn extra

profits. Online marketplaces and social media structures offer exceptional possibilities to show off and promote those products or services.

3. Rental Income: If massive families personal additional houses or have more region in their homes, they are capable of keep in mind renting it out for added earnings. Platforms like Airbnb have made it easier than ever to lease out spare rooms or maybe entire homes to vacationers or lengthy-time period tenants.

4. Passive Income: Investing in earnings-producing assets in conjunction with stocks, bonds, or real assets can offer a consistent glide of passive earnings. While this method may additionally require a few initial capital, it has the functionality to generate prolonged-time period wealth and monetary protection for large families.

five. Career Advancement: Big families with two jobs might also additionally find out opportunities for profession development or professional development. By acquiring new capabilities or certifications, people can characteristic themselves for promotions or higher-paying roles interior their respective fields.

6. Negotiating Salary: When starting a modern-day interest or at some stage in annual reviews, huge households should not shy away from negotiating their salaries. Researching enterprise requirements and imparting a sturdy case for increased repayment can bring about large income income.

7. Collaboration and Partnerships: Big families can find out collaboration possibilities with unique families or humans in comparable situations. Pooling assets, sharing costs, or beginning joint ventures can assist boom income and reduce economic burdens for in fact all of us worried.

By imposing the ones strategies for growing income, big households can take top notch steps towards conducting economic freedom. It is vital to maintain in thoughts that every own family's state of affairs is unique, and it can require a mixture of those techniques to discover the satisfactory approach. With self-control, perseverance, and smart economic planning, big families can triumph over their financial stressful situations and assemble a stable future for themselves and their cherished ones.

Reducing Expenses to Accelerate Debt Repayment

In the adventure in the path of debt compensation, one of the most effective strategies is to lessen costs. For large families with two jobs and large payments, finding ways to cut prices may be hard but now not now not feasible. By adopting a proactive approach and making small changes in your lifestyle and spending conduct, you can accelerate your debt compensation and regain manipulate over your rate variety.

Budgeting is the cornerstone of any a fulfillment debt reimbursement plan. Start via the use of developing a entire charge range that includes all belongings of earnings and fees. This will offer you with a smooth image of in which your cash goes and help understand areas in which you may make cuts. Review your rate variety often and alter it as critical to live on direction.

One of the number one areas to recall while decreasing expenses is your month-to-month payments. Look for strategies to shop on utilities, which incorporates turning off lights and electronics at the same time as no longer in use, adjusting the thermostat, and the usage of energy-inexperienced home equipment. Consider switching to a much less expensive mobile cellphone or net plan, or bundling offerings for additonal financial savings. Additionally, discover options for lowering coverage costs through manner of the utilization of purchasing round for higher charges.

Another big charge for big households is groceries. Cut down on food charges through the use of making plans meals earlier, developing a shopping for list, and purchasing for gadgets in bulk even as possible. Look for income and use coupons to maximize savings. Consider cooking at home extra frequently, packing lunches, and lowering eating out costs. Not amazing will this assist you hold coins, but it can moreover cause extra wholesome eating behavior.

Evaluate your amusement and leisure expenses. Assess your subscriptions and memberships, and cancel any that aren't vital. Look without value or low-price alternatives to luxurious sports activities, which include exploring close by parks, internet internet hosting game nights at domestic, or borrowing books and films from the library. By being aware about your spending on this vicinity, you may redirect the ones budget closer to debt repayment.

Finally, do not forget your transportation charges. Carpooling, using public transportation, or biking to art work can substantially lessen gas fees. If you've got were given multiple automobiles, evaluate whether downsizing to at least one or choosing more fuel-inexperienced alternatives is feasible. Additionally, discover alternatives for reducing preservation and coverage costs.

By implementing those techniques and being aware of your spending, you may reduce costs and boost up your debt reimbursement. Remember, every greenback stored is a step within the course of financial freedom. Stay dedicated on your goals, often anticipate another time your budget, and have a good time small victories alongside the manner. With energy of will and perseverance, you will triumph over your debts and construct a brighter economic future to your big family.

Chapter 8: Monitoring And Adjusting Your Budget

Tracking and Analyzing Expenses

Tracking and studying costs is a important step in handling your fee variety correctly. As a member of a large own family with jobs and large payments, it's miles important to have a solid knowledge of wherein your cash goes and the manner you may make the maximum of your tough-earned profits. In this subchapter, we're capable of find out the significance of monitoring and analyzing charges and provide sensible techniques that will help you stay on pinnacle of your budgeting desires.

Budgeting is the foundation of monetary fulfillment, and personal budgeting turns into even extra critical when you have a huge circle of relatives and a couple of earnings belongings. By tracking your costs, you benefit precious insights into your spending styles and might discover areas in which you can lessen yet again or make adjustments.

This facts can be a undertaking-changer in terms of reaching your monetary goals.

One vicinity in which monitoring and reading prices can be specially beneficial is journey budgeting. Planning family trips may be high-priced, however with the aid of carefully monitoring your charges, you may discover strategies to store cash with out compromising on exceptional. Whether it's far finding the excellent gives on flights and accommodation or setting aside a dedicated excursion fund, tracking costs permits you to make knowledgeable picks that align together with your family's finances.

Similarly, in phrases of wedding ceremony budgeting, tracking costs is critical to make certain that you live internal your selected spending limits. By preserving a close to eye in your prices, you can prioritize your wedding ceremony prices, allocate price range to every hassle of the event, and keep away from overspending. This degree of monetary interest will now not first-class help you propose a memorable wedding ceremony but also prevent any publish-bridal ceremony economic pressure.

Moreover, tracking and studying expenses play a critical role in retirement budgeting. As a huge own family with jobs and huge payments, it is important to devise for your retirement early on. By monitoring your costs, you can pick out out areas in which you can save extra and invest as it should be for a comfortable retirement. This subchapter will provide you with practical hints and strategies that will help you create a retirement finances that aligns at the side of your family's financial dreams.

Lastly, but absolutely now not least, monitoring and reading fees are critical in debt compensation budgeting. By intently monitoring your prices, you may allocate extra price range in the course of debt compensation, accelerate your development, and end up debt-free sooner. This subchapter will manual you thru developing a debt compensation plan and provide guidelines at the manner to stick with it.

In quit, monitoring and reading charges are essential to powerful budgeting. Whether you are handling private, circle of relatives, journey, bridal ceremony, retirement, or debt compensation budgets, know-how wherein your cash goes is essential to venture economic achievement. By implementing the strategies noted on this subchapter, you will benefit manipulate over your budget and pave the manner for a brighter monetary future to your massive family.

Making Necessary Adjustments to the Budget

Budgeting is an critical device for large families with two jobs and massive bills. It gives a roadmap for economic success and lets in you live heading in the right direction collectively collectively along with your financial dreams. However, as instances trade, it's miles vital to make important modifications for your budget to make certain that it stays effective and applicable.

One region in which adjustments may be important is private budgeting. As your circle of relatives grows and evolves, your dreams and priorities may additionally alternate. It is important to regularly evaluation your personal price range to account for any new expenses or adjustments in profits. This should embody adjusting your discretionary spending, reallocating price range in the direction of training or healthcare charges, or saving for future goals together with a down charge on a residence or a infant's college education.

Family budgeting is a few different vicinity that calls for periodic changes. As kids growth, their goals and sports activities may also moreover additionally become more pricey. It is important to devise for the ones modifications through the usage of revisiting your charge variety and making critical changes. This could in all likelihood contain increasing your allocation for childcare fees, extracurricular sports, or instructional property. Additionally, as your own family dynamics trade, you could want to adjust your charge range to residence new family contributors or changes in dwelling arrangements.

Travel budgeting is every other vicinity of interest that requires adjustments. While adventure can be a precious revel in for big families, it is able to moreover be high priced. It is vital to set realistic goals and allocate budget consequently. If your charge range does not permit for extravagant vacations, don't forget more low cost alternatives collectively with camping journeys or exploring close by factors of hobby. By making adjustments for your tour price range, you could nonetheless experience awesome time collectively along with your family without breaking the financial group.

Wedding budgeting is a big economic attention for lots massive families. As weddings can be high priced affairs, it's miles crucial to devise and make essential changes for your rate variety. This may also include prioritizing fees, negotiating issuer contracts, or exploring DIY options. By being aware of your fee variety and making essential changes, you could create a memorable bridal ceremony experience without amassing immoderate debt.

Retirement budgeting is vital for prolonged-time period economic protection. As you approach retirement age, it is important to check your charge variety and make vital changes to ensure a snug retirement. This may want to contain developing your retirement monetary savings contributions, downsizing your dwelling arrangements, or exploring extra income streams.

Lastly, debt repayment budgeting is of most significance for large households with jobs and big payments. If you're sporting massive debt, it's far essential to allocate part of your fee variety in the direction of debt reimbursement. By making important changes and prioritizing debt repayment, you may artwork inside the path of monetary freedom and decrease the burden of debt.

In end, making crucial changes on your rate variety is important for big households with jobs and large payments. By often reviewing and adjusting your fee variety, you could make sure that it stays powerful and aligned along side your converting desires and financial goals. Whether it's far private budgeting, own family budgeting, journey budgeting, wedding ceremony budgeting, retirement budgeting, or debt compensation budgeting, staying proactive and making crucial adjustments will set you at the course to financial achievement.

Staying Motivated and Committed to the Budgeting Process

Budgeting is a important device for massive households with jobs and massive bills. It allows you to take manage of your budget, prioritize your spending, and art work inside the course of your financial goals. However, sticking to a budget may be difficult, specially while confronted with surprising charges or temptations to overspend. In this subchapter, we can find out powerful strategies to help you stay prompted and committed to the budgeting approach.

One of the maximum critical additives of staying stimulated is placing practical dreams. Begin through figuring out your economic objectives, whether or not it's far paying off debt, saving for a circle of relatives vacation, or making plans for retirement. Break down those goals into smaller, doable milestones that can be tracked and celebrated alongside the way. This will help you live inspired and focused in your prolonged-time period monetary success.

Another key method is to incorporate the complete circle of relatives within the budgeting technique. By developing a feel of shared duty, anyone will become liable for their spending behavior. Sit down collectively and speak the economic dreams as a family. Encourage open and honest verbal exchange about the price range, and contain children in age-suitable discussions about cash control. This will no longer simplest beautify your own family's financial basis but moreover domesticate responsible spending behavior in the greater younger era.

Additionally, locating techniques to make budgeting fun can notably boom your motivation. Consider the use of budgeting apps or software software that provide visible representations of your development. Seeing your debt lower or financial savings growth may be fairly motivating. You also can create rewards for assembly unique milestones, together with a own family day ride or a small treat. Celebrating your financial successes will help you live dedicated to the budgeting machine.

Lastly, keep in mind that setbacks are a natural a part of the adventure. Unexpected charges or moments of vulnerable point are sure to appear. Instead of having discouraged, view the ones moments as analyzing opportunities. Reflect on what went wrong and the way you may prevent similar situations in the destiny. Stay bendy and alter your price variety as needed.

In surrender, staying advocated and devoted to the budgeting method is vital for big households with jobs and big bills. By placing practical desires, concerning the family, making budgeting a laugh, and embracing setbacks as studying possibilities, you can successfully navigate the worrying conditions and advantage financial stability. Remember, your price range is a device that empowers you to take control of your economic destiny, and with power of will and perseverance, you can obtain your monetary goals.

Chapter 9: Resources And Tools For Effective Budgeting

Recommended Budgeting Apps and Software

In this virtual age, coping with your rate range has in no way been easier. With the wide array of budgeting apps and software program software program to be had, huge families with jobs and huge payments can now take control in their fee variety with out difficulty and performance. In this subchapter, we're capable of find out a number of the advocated budgeting apps and software program application that cater in particular to the desires of individuals and households going through financial annoying situations.

1. Mint: Mint is a complete budgeting app that allows you to tune your spending, create budgets, and set financial dreams. It robotically categorizes your transactions, provides custom designed cash-saving recommendations, and sends alerts whilst you exceed your budget. With Mint, you can

gain a clear compare of your monetary fitness and with out issue pick out out regions in which you may lessen lower again on costs.

2. YNAB (You Need a Budget): YNAB is a popular budgeting app that makes a speciality of supporting you allocate your earnings to precise lessons and prioritize your monetary desires. It encourages you to provide every dollar a interest and affords real-time updates in your spending conduct. YNAB additionally gives educational assets and assist that will help you construct a sturdy financial basis.

3. EveryDollar: Created by means of the use of financial professional Dave Ramsey, EveryDollar follows a 0-based definitely budgeting technique. It lets in you to allocate every dollar of your earnings to top notch instructions, ensuring which you have a plan for every cent. The app moreover offers a visible example of your fee variety through charts and graphs, making it smooth to music your improvement.

four. Personal Capital: Personal Capital is not most effective a budgeting app however moreover a complete monetary manage device. It permits you to tune your costs, show your investments, and plan for retirement. With its retirement planner feature, you can set economic financial savings dreams and calculate how an awful lot you want to keep to gain your desired retirement life-style.

5. Goodbudget: Goodbudget is right for families looking to control their finances collectively. It makes use of the envelope budgeting method, wherein you allocate cash to fantastic digital envelopes for extraordinary prices. This app allows you to sync your finances with extraordinary family individuals, ensuring honestly all people is at the same web page in phrases of economic goals and spending behavior.

Whether you are budgeting for personal charges, circle of relatives needs, excursion, weddings, or debt repayment, the ones encouraged budgeting apps and software program can provide you with the gear and insights you want to benefit financial balance. By utilising those virtual belongings, huge families with jobs and massive bills can navigate their economic annoying situations with self perception and make knowledgeable alternatives that allows you to motive a brighter economic destiny.

Online Resources for Financial Education and Support

In this digital technology, in which information is only a click on away, it has grow to be less difficult than ever to access property that might assist us decorate our economic literacy and control our fee variety efficaciously. This subchapter will discover the severa on line property available for people and households seeking out monetary schooling and manual, catering mainly to large households with jobs and large payments.

Budgeting is the muse of monetary balance, and happily, there are numerous net net websites and apps dedicated to this example rely. Websites like Mint, YNAB (You Need A Budget), and Personal Capital provide unfastened budgeting device that allow you to tune your prices, set financial dreams, and create practical budgets on your circle of relatives. These systems offer insightful economic recommendation and offer personalized guidelines primarily based definitely for your spending patterns.

Personal budgeting is a important trouble of coping with your price range, and systems which incorporates PocketGuard and Goodbudget can be immensely useful. With the ones apps, you may create customized budgets, track your profits and costs, and gather indicators even as you exceed your finances limits. They moreover offer abilities like bill reminders and debt payoff calculators, which might be particularly useful for huge families with more than one financial responsibilities.

Family budgeting requires cautious making plans and coordination, and net internet web sites like EveryDollar and Honeydue can simplify this device. These structures will let you create shared budgets collectively together with your accomplice or family participants, making sure clearly everybody stays on the equal internet page financially. You can track joint fees, set economic financial savings dreams, or even assign duties to preserve each unique accountable.

While dealing with every day charges is vital, it's also important to devise for primary existence activities like journey, weddings, and retirement. Websites like Travel Budget and The Knot offer whole courses and tools to help massive households plan and charge variety for vacations and weddings, respectively. For retirement planning, resources like AARP and Vanguard offer instructional substances, retirement calculators, and personalized recommendation to help you strong a cushty future.

Finally, for those struggling with debt repayment, web sites like Debt.Org and National Foundation for Credit Counseling (NFCC) provide precious data and property. These systems offer debt control plans, credit score rating counseling offerings, and guidance on negotiating with creditors, empowering huge families to regain manage of their fee range.

In stop, the internet is a treasure trove of belongings for monetary training and assist. Big families with jobs and massive payments can take advantage of online tools, apps, and net websites to improve their budgeting and financial manage skills, plan for primary existence activities, and deal with debt efficaciously. By harnessing the power of those online belongings, households can reap economic stability and set themselves up for a steady destiny.

Seeking Professional Assistance for Debt Repayment

When it involves dealing with debt repayment, huge families with jobs and big bills often discover themselves overwhelmed and uncertain of in which to start. It's essential to recollect which you do not have to face this undertaking by myself. Seeking expert help can offer you with the guidance and assist you need to create a strong debt reimbursement plan and regain manage of your charge range.

One of the primary steps in looking for expert assistance is to find out a incredible credit score rating counseling organisation. These corporations are committed to supporting people and families navigate their manner out of debt. They can provide you with valuable advice and assets to govern your price range more effectively.

A credit score counselor will work cautiously with you to assess your monetary state of affairs, which encompass your profits, costs, and exquisite money owed. This assessment will assist them benefit a smooth facts of your monetary desires and boom a personalized debt reimbursement plan tailored on your specific occasions.

Additionally, credit score rating counselors can negotiate collectively with your creditors on your behalf. They have the records and revel in to speak successfully with creditors, aiming to reduce interest expenses, waive costs, or create more conceivable fee plans. This allow you to preserve coins and boost up your debt reimbursement adventure.

In addition to credit score counseling companies, you could additionally take into account working with a economic planner or advertising and marketing consultant. These specialists can offer entire economic advice, assisting you create a price range that prioritizes debt reimbursement at the same time as additionally addressing your different monetary desires, at the side of saving for retirement or planning for a massive circle of relatives excursion.

Remember, searching for professional assist does now not recommend you've got failed or are incapable of managing your rate range It in reality manner which you are taking proactive steps to enhance your monetary scenario and solid a brighter future on your circle of relatives.

In conclusion, looking for professional help for debt compensation may be a recreation-changer for big households with jobs and large bills. With the guidance and help of credit score rating counseling companies or economic advisors, you could create sensible finances, negotiate with lenders, and increase a strong reimbursement plan. By taking this step, you are empowering yourself to overcome debt and gain financial stability for your own family.

Chapter 10: Changing Your Financial Mindset

In the adventure towards mastering the artwork of budgeting, one can't underestimate the strength of mind-set. Our ideals and attitudes approximately cash shape our financial alternatives and ultimately decide our success in budgeting. In this financial disaster, we are capable of find out the significance of converting your economic thoughts-set and provide sensible strategies to cultivate a excessive wonderful and proactive mindset closer to your rate range.

The first step inside the direction of changing your monetary mindset is to end up privy to any limiting beliefs you can have approximately cash. These ideals often stem from our upbringing, societal conditioning, or past opinions. They can seem as thoughts which include "I will in no way be able to preserve enough" or "I am not right with coins." By acknowledging and hard those beliefs, we can begin to reframe our wondering and open ourselves as plenty as new opportunities.

To conquer restricting beliefs about coins, it's far critical to understand that they may be not set in stone. They are honestly thoughts that we've were given standard as reality. By thinking the validity of those beliefs and analyzing the evidence that allows or contradicts them, we can begin to dismantle their power over us. It may be useful to are trying to find for aid from a therapist or train who focuses on coins thoughts-set to manual you via this technique.

Once you have got recognized and challenged your limiting ideals, it's time to domesticate a nice and proactive mind-set inside the path of your rate range. This includes adopting new behavior and strategies that align along with your monetary dreams. Here are 4 steps to help you increase a powerful cash mindset:

1.   Forgive your Financial Mistakes: We all make errors with regards to cash. Instead of living on beyond failures, it's far important to

forgive your self and research from them. Use those research as lessons to inform your destiny monetary picks.

2. Set Financial Goals: Having clear dreams gives you some aspect to art work closer to and allows you stay motivated. Set every quick-term and lengthy-term financial desires which may be particular, measurable, capability, relevant, and time-sure (SMART). Write them down and frequently evaluation your improvement.

three. Optimize Your Budget for Happiness: Budgeting is not just about proscribing your self; it's far approximately aligning your spending together with your values and priorities. Take the time to assess your charges and determine what absolutely brings you joy and fulfillment. Allocate your assets for that reason and reduce returned on needless charges that don't make contributions for your popular well-being.

4. Inform Yourself approximately Money: Knowledge is energy with regards to non-

public finance. Educate your self about budgeting, making an investment, and different economic topics. Read books, pay attention to podcasts, and attend workshops or seminars to enlarge your economic literacy. The extra , the greater confident and empowered you will feel in coping with your cash.

Now, allow me percentage a private experience that illustrates the transformative strength of changing your economic mind-set. Several years in the past, I decided myself trapped in a cycle of overspending and debt. I had generally believed that I changed into destined to battle with cash and that financial freedom became out of gain for someone like me. However, ultimately, I had a 2nd of readability. I asked myself, "What do I want my life to appear like after I have cash underneath control and jogging for me?"

This query sparked a profound shift in my questioning. I realized that I had the power to change my monetary scenario if I even have turn out to be willing to change my mindset. I began out out to task my restricting ideals and replace them with empowering mind. I forgave myself for past errors and set bold financial desires. I optimized my finances to prioritize memories and investments that delivered me actual happiness. And most importantly, I devoted to continuously teaching myself about coins and personal finance.

Over time, my monetary scenario progressed extensively. I paid off my money owed, started out out saving diligently, and even commenced making an funding in opportunities that aligned with my desires. But more than that, I professional a newfound sense of empowerment and manipulate over my financial future. Changing my economic attitude come to be the catalyst that transformed my relationship with coins and set me on the path to financial achievement.

Changing your monetary mind-set is a crucial step towards gaining knowledge of the art work of budgeting. By becoming privy to and difficult your restricting beliefs, you could open your self up to new opportunities. Cultivating a powerful and proactive mind-set towards your finances consists of forgiving beyond errors, setting clean goals, optimizing your price variety for happiness, and constantly teaching yourself approximately coins. Remember, your mind-set shapes your truth, and with the right thoughts-set, you could gain economic freedom and create the life you preference.

Setting SMART Financial Goals

Chapter 11: Setting Smart Financial Goals

In the journey in the course of financial achievement, putting dreams is a crucial step. Without a smooth vision of what we want to advantage, it becomes hard to stay brought about and targeted on our financial endeavors. However, not all desires are created equal. To genuinely maintain close the artwork of budgeting, it is important to set SMART financial dreams.

But what makes a cause SMART? SMART stands for Specific, Measurable, Achievable, Relevant, and Time-superb. By incorporating those elements into our financial dreams, we growth our possibilities of achievement and create a roadmap within the course of a brighter financial future.

Setting economic desires can be a effective motivator. When we've were given some issue specific to try for, it becomes much less difficult to stay disciplined and make the crucial sacrifices to accumulate our objectives. Whether it's far saving for a down charge on a house, paying off scholar loans, or constructing a retirement nest egg, having a smooth monetary intention offers us a feel of purpose and course.

Short-term and long-time period desires play a important position in our economic adventure. Short-time period dreams are folks that may be finished inner a five-three hundred and sixty five days window, on the identical time as long-time period dreams make bigger past that time frame. Short-term desires also can include searching for a ultra-modern car or paying down debt, whilst lengthy-term goals may additionally need to comprise saving for retirement, funding your kid's training, or searching for a holiday home.

To create a roadmap for engaging in our monetary dreams, we need to take a look at some essential steps. First and maximum critical, we want to apprehend in which we currently stand financially. This self-cognizance lets in us to assess our situation realistically and make knowledgeable choices approximately our dreams. Once we've were given a clean knowledge of our economic function, we are able to skip without delay to the subsequent step.

Setting goals is the next important step in our monetary roadmap. By putting particular and measurable desires, we deliver ourselves a aim to motive for. Instead of vaguely hoping to shop cash, we're capable of set a specific quantity that we want to save indoors a certain time-frame. This specificity lets in us to song our development and make changes along the way.

Creating an movement plan is the 0.33 step in the course of accomplishing our financial goals. This plan outlines the stairs we need to take to gain our goals. It may additionally additionally furthermore consist of decreasing expenses, growing earnings, or making an investment appropriately. By breaking down our dreams into actionable steps, we make them more conceivable and boom our possibilities of success.

Equipping ourselves with the right equipment is vital for staying heading in the right direction. Whether it's far budgeting apps, spreadsheets, or financial planners, those gear can help us display our improvement and make knowledgeable monetary picks. By leveraging era and belongings, we're capable of make our monetary adventure smoother and extra green.

Staying recommended and responsible to our goals may be hard, but it is not no longer feasible. There are numerous strategies we're capable of lease to maintain ourselves on target. First and important, we need to be brutally sincere with ourselves. This method acknowledging our weaknesses, temptations, and regions in which we will be predisposed to sabotage our improvement. By being aware of the ones elements, we are capable of boom strategies to conquer them.

Committing to a schedule is each other effective manner to live inspired and accountable. By placing unique instances for reviewing our development, making changes, and celebrating milestones, we create a experience of structure and region in our financial journey. This ordinary take a look at-in ensures that we stay focused and devoted to our dreams.

Creating micro-goals can also help us live inspired. Instead of completely focusing at the save you end result, breaking our dreams into smaller, doable milestones lets in us to have fun our development alongside the way. These mini-victories function reminders of our skills and preserve us prompted to keep pushing in advance.

Having an responsibility accomplice can be a recreation-changer in our economic journey. This person may be a pal, family member, or maybe a financial instruct who holds us accountable to our dreams. By sharing our improvement, challenges, and victories with a person else, we create a experience of outside responsibility and resource.

Overcoming self-sabotage is a essential issue of staying brought about and accountable. We all have moments of weak point and temptation, but spotting the ones patterns and growing techniques to overcome them is important. Whether it's miles warding off useless charges, enforcing spending limits, or education aware spending, we are able to take manage of our monetary options and stay on course.

Understanding our "why" is a powerful motivator. When we've got got a deep-rooted motive for pursuing our financial goals, it turns into less difficult to stay committed and centered. Whether it is supplying a higher future for our circle of relatives, accomplishing monetary independence, or pursuing our passions, know-how our why gives us the pressure to maintain pushing forward.

Finally, celebrating each little win is critical for preserving motivation and momentum. Every step within the route of our financial goals is a victory nicely well worth acknowledging and celebrating. By recognizing our progress, we red meat up tremendous conduct and build self perception in our functionality to gain our huge goals.

Setting SMART monetary goals is a essential step toward getting to know the artwork of budgeting. By incorporating specificity, measurability, achievability, relevance, and time-effective factors into our desires, we boom our probabilities of fulfillment. Additionally, staying prompted and responsible via techniques consisting of self-honesty, scheduling, micro-goals, responsibility companions, overcoming self-sabotage, know-how our why, and celebrating victories, ensures that we live at the proper music and gain our economic goals. So, let us embark in this journey of setting SMART financial desires and pave the way for a brighter and extra wealthy future.

Creating an Effective Budget Framework

Chapter 12: Creating An Effective Budget Framework

As we delve deeper into the area of budgeting, it becomes evident that locating the right budgeting device is crucial for monetary fulfillment. With severa strategies and techniques to be had, people need to discover a framework that aligns with their particular activities and dreams. In this bankruptcy, we will find out the wonderful budgeting techniques and communicate the way to create a flexible and adaptable price variety framework.

One of the maximum famous budgeting techniques is the 0-based totally price variety. This technique revolves across the principle that income minus fees want to identical zero. By assigning every greenback a particular motive, individuals can gain a complete know-how of their monetary state of affairs. The 0-primarily based certainly budgeting approach calls for careful planning and interest of each fee, making sure that every greenback is accounted for.

Another effective budgeting approach is the pay-your self-first finances. This technique prioritizes saving via the use of allocating part of your income to monetary financial savings in advance than each different charges. By making saving a non-negotiable element of your price range, you can construct a robust financial foundation and art work within the route of achieving your lengthy-term dreams.

For individuals who pick a greater tangible technique, the envelope gadget rate variety can be pretty effective. This method consists of dividing your cash into exquisite envelopes, each representing a specific cost category. By physical retaining aside your coins, you advantage a visible representation of your spending limits and can higher tune your fees.

The 50/30/20 rate variety is a few other famous technique that divides your profits into 3 education: 50% for wishes, 30% for goals, and 20% for financial financial savings and debt reimbursement. This technique offers a balanced framework that lets in for each responsible spending and saving.

Lastly, the no-price variety price range is a manner that makes a speciality of monitoring and analyzing your spending behavior without constantly assigning precise dollar portions to each magnificence. This method can be useful for those who choose a more flexible budgeting tool that emphasizes attention and aware spending.

When allocating price range for brilliant instructions and fees, severa factors want to be taken into consideration. Firstly, it's miles important to decide your usual spending necessities. This may be done with the resource of studying your past spending conduct or making informed estimates based totally to your modern-day financial situation. By having a clean knowledge of your spending desires, you could allocate finances consequently.

Identifying investment techniques is every different vital step in developing an powerful price range framework. This entails considering severa property of income, together with salaries, investments, or facet hustles. By diversifying your profits streams, you can create a more solid monetary basis and allocate finances extra correctly.

Once you have got decided your ordinary spending necessities and identified investment techniques, it's far essential to allocate your price range via manner of branch or class. This lets in for better agency and ensures that each fee is accounted for. By assigning specific dollar portions to every beauty, you can show your spending more efficaciously and make changes as preferred.

To ensure your charge variety framework is flexible and adaptable, it's miles essential to layout a device for monitoring spend. This may be executed via the use of budgeting apps or equipment. There are severa encouraged budgeting apps to be had, which incorporates YNAB, Empower Personal Dashboard, Mint, and Goodbudget. These apps provide abilties that help track spending, set financial desires, and offer insights into your frequently going on monetary health.

Furthermore, incorporating a strategic budgeting approach like Zero-Based Budgeting (ZBB) can enhance the capability and flexibility of your rate variety. ZBB requires a smooth evaluation of all costs for the period of every budgeting cycle, taking into account ordinary restructuring based totally totally on changes in interest. This approach guarantees that your price range remains aligned along facet your monetary desires and can adapt to unexpected situations.

Chapter 13: Tracking Income And Expenses

In the hunt to master the artwork of budgeting, one cannot underestimate the importance of tracking each penny. It is thru this meticulous monitoring that we're capable of advantage a deeper records of our monetary behavior and make informed alternatives approximately our spending. By retaining a report of every greenback earned and spent, we are able to find out styles and find out areas in which fees may be reduced, main us inside the direction of a more balanced and financially solid destiny.

To embark in this journey of tracking our earnings and charges, it's far critical to have the right gear at our disposal. Luckily, there are various effective system and apps to be had in the market that can simplify this technique. Mint, EveryDollar, YNAB, LendingTree, Expensify, and Truebill are only a few examples of these valuable assets. These device not first-rate assist us tune our earnings and charges however moreover provide insightful evaluation and visible representations of our monetary information, making it less complex to discover dispositions and regions for development.

Once armed with the important gear, it's time to delve into the intricacies of reading our spending patterns. This step calls for us to take a practical take a look at our contemporary conduct and confront the truth of our economic choices. One effective method is to examine our financial institution account and credit score card facts for the beyond numerous months. This exercise allows us to look the bigger photo and gain a whole information of our spending conduct. Alternatively, signing up for a personal economic control tool can offer us with a easy and concise study of our spending, doing away with the need for guide assessment. Whichever approach we pick out, the key's to be thorough and honest with ourselves as we dissect our economic options.

Consistency is the cornerstone of a success budgeting, and monitoring our profits and charges is not any exception. To stay regular, we want to establish a ordinary and persist with it. The first step on this technique is to create a rate variety. Without a rate range, tracking expenses becomes a futile exercise. Once we have a finances in vicinity, we can then track our income diligently. Every time a paycheck is to be had in, it should be recorded within the income section of our rate variety. Similarly, each rate ought to be tracked. This includes each crucial fees and discretionary spending. By placing a regular rhythm for monitoring, we make certain that no price slips through the cracks, allowing us to have an entire and accurate photograph of our monetary situation.

Tracking our profits and charges isn't virtually a secular undertaking; it's far a powerful tool for figuring out regions of improvement in our price range. Regularly monitoring our spending gives us a smooth and accurate picture of wherein our cash goes. It allows us to discover patterns and dispositions that can have prolonged gone left out in any other case. Armed with this information, we're able to then make knowledgeable alternatives approximately our financial priorities and reallocate our sources for this reason. By the use of a rate variety, we can make certain that all our payments are accounted for and that our financial goals are inside reach.

Tracking our profits and costs is an crucial step in the direction of studying the artwork of budgeting. It allows us to gain a deeper know-how of our financial behavior, select out regions for development, and make knowledgeable picks about our spending. With the right equipment and a everyday technique, we can take manage of our charge range and pave the way for a more strong and wealthy future. So let us embark on this adventure of tracking, armed with strength of will and a preference for financial freedom. The path to mastery awaits us.

Income Maximization Strategies

Chapter 14: Income Maximization Strategies

In the pursuit of economic balance and prosperity, people often discover themselves exploring severa belongings of income beyond their number one task. This bankruptcy delves into the vicinity of income maximization strategies, supplying insights and steerage on the way to growth one's incomes ability. From passive income mind to negotiation techniques and private improvement investments, this financial ruin desires to equip readers with the device essential to understand the art work of maximizing their earnings.

The quest for added sources of earnings starts with a attitude shift closer to embracing opportunities that cross past traditional employment. One such street is dropshipping, a way that permits human beings to run an internet save with out the need for stock. This passive income idea allows marketers to earn coins from everywhere, regardless of restrained preliminary capital. Another preference is growing a print-on-call for save, in which human beings can layout and sell custom merchandise with out the load of producing and shipping logistics. Additionally, selling virtual products, teaching on-line courses, becoming a blogger, promoting home made items, and jogging an companion marketing and advertising business organisation are all feasible income maximization strategies properly really worth exploring.

However, the adventure in the route of profits maximization does not prevent with identifying potential assets of income. It is equally essential to boom the talents and expertise important to negotiate sales increases or freelance prices effectively. When drawing close such negotiations, it is critical to determine the popular boom and make sure it is large sufficient to warrant a prolonged period even as not having to ask again. By tackling negotiations with customers one after the other, starting with the lowest-paying one, people can construct their self warranty and increase their opportunities of achievement. Even if the preliminary attempts do now not yield the famous final consequences, the experience gained will show treasured in destiny negotiations.

Investing in non-public and professional improvement is each other pivotal aspect of profits maximization. Continuously gaining knowledge of and teaching oneself is a effective device for developing incomes potential. Attending workshops, seminars, and conferences can offer human beings with new facts and insights, at the same time as self-have a have a look at lets in for the growth of understanding. Reading books is a timeless method of acquiring facts, and it's miles critical to prioritize every breadth and intensity in a single's studying options. Furthermore, honing current abilties and acquiring new ones is a surefire manner to beautify marketability. Seeking out a mentor who can provide steering and recommendation can also be immensely beneficial in navigating the complexities of income maximization.

To illustrate the functionality of income maximization techniques, it's far truely well really worth exploring fulfillment memories and examples. One such example is the concept of passive income, which involves making an initial funding that generates earnings with out requiring everyday paintings. Whether thru making an investment in monetary property or beginning a employer, passive earnings has the functionality to offer long-time period economic stability. While it could require strive and power of will earlier, the rewards can be large and ongoing.

However, it is vital to renowned the capacity worrying conditions and dangers related to income maximization. One not unusual pitfall is the temptation to prioritize sales over income. While sacrificing quick-time period profits to boom sales can also seem appealing, it's far an unsustainable exercise that can purpose prolonged-time period business business enterprise failure. Balancing the pursuit of income with retaining a healthful earnings margin is crucial for sustainable income maximization. Additionally, it's far vital to bear in mind of the dangers related to effective earnings maximization techniques, which include the volatility of investments or the capability saturation of high quality markets. A entire information of the dangers concerned lets in human beings to make knowledgeable selections and mitigate capability setbacks.

Chapter 15: Minimizing Debt And Maximizing Savings

In the journey within the route of monetary balance, there are critical factors that must be mastered: minimizing debt and maximizing economic financial savings. These pillars work hand in hand, as decreasing debt allows for more price range to be allocated within the course of monetary monetary financial savings. In this bankruptcy, we are capable of find out strategies and suggestions to help people reap this sensitive stability.

One of the best strategies for paying off debt successfully is the snowball approach. This technique consists of tackling the smallest debt first, paying it off as rapid as possible. By focusing on the smallest debt, human beings enjoy a experience of achievement and motivation, propelling them earlier in their debt repayment adventure. While paying off the smallest debt, it's far vital to hold making minimal bills on all extraordinary money owed. Once the smallest debt is cleared, the more price variety can then be redirected in the route of the following biggest debt. This technique not most effective minimizes debt however additionally builds momentum, making the technique seem a good deal much less daunting.

Alternatively, there may be the debt avalanche method, which prioritizes paying off the largest or maximum interest fee debt first. Similar to the snowball technique, minimal bills are made on all different debts. By centered on the debt with the very top notch hobby rate, human beings can keep cash ultimately via manner of way of decreasing the quantity of interest accrued. This approach requires region and a protracted-time period perspective, as it may take greater time to see enormous development. However, the monetary blessings may be considerable.

Another choice to recollect is debt consolidation. This consists of combining multiple money owed proper right into a single mortgage with a lower hobby fee. Debt consolidation can simplify the compensation technique through streamlining a couple of bills into one. It can also likely lessen the general hobby paid, making it less complicated to manipulate debt and allocate more rate variety towards financial savings. However, it's far important to carefully examine the terms and conditions of any consolidation offer to make sure it aligns collectively together with your financial desires.

While minimizing debt is important, constructing an emergency fund and saving for the future are in addition critical. One effective method for accomplishing that is putting in vicinity routine transfers from your checking account for your financial savings account. By automating this approach, you make sure steady contributions on your monetary financial financial savings without the want for normal manual intervention. This approach permits you to decide the quantity and frequency of transfers, presenting flexibility even as retaining a disciplined technique to saving.

In addition to automatic transfers, there are first-rate hints and strategies to assist individuals store coins on normal charges. Joining loyalty applications can provide rewards and discounts, maximizing the rate of your purchases. Utilizing coins-returned credit score score gambling playing cards permits you to earn cash over again for your every day spending. Canceling subscriptions that aren't being carried out can free up greater rate range for monetary savings. Embracing a do-it-yourself mentality each time possible also can lead to massive charge economic financial savings. Setting up automatic invoice payments ensures nicely timed payments and avoids vain overdue charges. Switching monetary company bills to take benefit of higher hobby rates or lower prices can also make contributions to lengthy-time period financial financial savings. By carefully scrutinizing your spending conduct and searching out more money on your charge range, you may become aware of areas wherein charges can be decreased or eliminated.

To useful resource within the technique of minimizing debt and maximizing economic financial savings, there are various endorsed assets and gear to be had. Mint, YNAB (You Need a Budget), Goodbudget, and EveryDollar are only a few examples of budgeting apps and systems that can assist in tracking prices, putting economic dreams, and coping with debt compensation. These equipment offer a whole assessment of your monetary state of affairs, deliberating better selection-making and extended responsibility.

Balancing debt reimbursement and economic financial savings desires can be a difficult assignment. It requires cautious consideration of priorities and a strategic technique. One choice is to prioritize paying off the first-class-hobby debt first, as this may shop the maximum coins in the end. Another method is to attention on clearing the smallest debt first, offering a sense of achievement and motivation. Alternatively, individuals can prioritize the debts that have the most big effect on their credit score rating score. This technique guarantees that their creditworthiness is maintained at the same time as nevertheless making progress in the route of debt reduce price.

In a few times, debt consolidation can be a likely answer for humans with a couple of high-interest money owed. By consolidating those money owed right into a single loan with a decrease interest price, humans can simplify their repayment manner and probably shop coins on interest. However, it is critical to carefully study the terms and conditions of any consolidation offer to make sure it aligns collectively at the side of your economic dreams and does now not bring about more fees or costs.

Minimizing debt and maximizing financial savings are crucial additives of engaging in financial balance. By enforcing techniques at the side of the snowball or debt avalanche approach, people can correctly pay off their money owed. Building an emergency fund and saving for the future may be facilitated through computerized transfers and aware spending conduct. Utilizing belongings and device which encompass budgeting apps can offer valuable insights and guidance alongside the manner. Balancing debt compensation and savings desires requires careful interest and prioritization. Ultimately, with the aid of using taking proactive steps inside the course of minimizing debt and maximizing financial savings, humans can pave the way toward a steady monetary future.

Budgeting for Families

Chapter 16: Budgeting For Families

In the chaotic realm of family lifestyles, dealing with price range can regularly feel like an insurmountable assignment. Balancing the dreams of every member of the family whilst striving to acquire commonplace goals requires cautious planning and a company hold near at the paintings of budgeting. In this bankruptcy, we are able to discover techniques and strategies that can assist households navigate the complex panorama of financial management, making sure a harmonious and rich future.

One of the first steps in effective own family budgeting is to study your spending. Take a near check your expenses and discover areas wherein you can cut returned or make modifications. By doing so, you may create a price range that reflects your own family's priorities and values. Additionally, constructing a financial economic savings buffer is crucial for economic balance. Set apart a part of your profits each month create an emergency fund that would offer a protection net in the course of surprising times.

To effectively control your charge variety as a own family, it is crucial to determine what you're saving for. Whether it's a dream vacation, a down rate on a house, or your children's education, placing clean goals will help you live targeted and inspired. Set a very last date for each purpose to create a enjoy of urgency and hold yourselves responsible.

Creating a separate fee-free financial agency account also can be useful. This account want to be wonderful out of your primary account and dedicated simply to monetary savings. By preserving your financial savings separate, you can avoid the temptation to dip into them for day by day fees. This clean step could make a big distinction in your ability to advantage your economic desires.

Teaching kids about coins and budgeting is an crucial problem of circle of relatives financial control. By instilling the ones talents early on, you're equipping them with the device they need to navigate the complex international of private finance. One powerful approach is to manipulate an allowance. By giving your kids a tough and speedy amount of money every week or month, you could train them about budgeting, saving, and making choices with their cash.

Engaging in open conversations approximately cash is also crucial. By discussing economic topics along side your kids, you can assist them enlarge a healthy dating with cash and recognize its charge. Creating a novice rate variety together can be a fun and educational interest. By associated with your kids inside the budgeting way, they may benefit a deeper appreciation for the significance of monetary making plans.

Leading with the useful resource of instance is some other effective way to teach youngsters about coins. Show them the way you manipulate your own finances and make responsible choices. Money video games and activities can also be a awesome way to make studying approximately cash exciting. By incorporating play into the procedure, you can instill precious schooling whilst developing lasting reminiscences.

As families try and balance man or woman wishes with family desires, the 50/30/20 price range can function a beneficial framework. This charge range splits your profits into 3 training: 50% for goals, which encompass groceries, housing, utilities, and infant care; 30% for desires, which consist of journey, provides, and ingesting out; and 20% for saving, emergency finances, retirement, and debt compensation. By allocating your income on this way, you could ensure that each individual dreams and circle of relatives goals are given identical hobby.

Finding the right tools and property to useful resource your family's budgeting efforts is critical. There are severa budgeting apps and software software to be had that may streamline the system and provide precious insights. Mint, Goodbudget, EveryDollar, and

YNAB are just a few examples of those equipment. Additionally, spreadsheets can be a easy yet effective way to song your costs and monitor your progress.

While budgeting for households can be immensely worthwhile, it isn't with out its annoying conditions. One not unusual obstacle is being indecisive about price range. It is vital to make clear and knowledgeable alternatives to avoid unnecessary pressure and confusion. Impulse searching for also can derail even the most nicely-intentioned price variety. By education restraint and mindful spending, you can keep away from falling into this trap.

Having economic dreams is crucial for effective budgeting. Without easy desires, it is easy to lose sight of the larger photograph and make options that aren't aligned collectively together with your circle of relatives's lengthy-term aspirations. It is likewise vital to use the proper budgeting method that fits your circle of relatives's needs and options. Finding a way that works for you'll make the budgeting approach more manageable and sustainable.

Fear of handling debt may be a tremendous hurdle for households. However, it's miles crucial to confront this worry head-on and growth a plan to manipulate and cast off debt. By addressing this trouble, you could alleviate monetary strain and create a stable foundation for future monetary achievement.

Another mission that households regularly face is eating out too frequently. Dining out can short drain your price range, so it is critical to set limits and prioritize home-cooked meals. By making plans your meals earlier and regarding the whole own family inside the cooking approach, you could hold coins while gambling remarkable time collectively.

Consistency is prime on the subject of budgeting. It is crucial to set up a habitual and hold on with it. By constantly monitoring your charges, reviewing your charge variety, and making important changes, you could keep economic balance and accumulate your desires.

Mastering the artwork of budgeting as a circle of relatives requires careful planning, open verbal exchange, and a dedication to lengthy-time period economic dreams. By implementing the techniques and techniques stated on this chapter, you may navigate the complexities of circle of relatives fee range with self belief and create a wealthy destiny on your circle of relatives. Remember, financial manipulate isn't always just about numbers; it's miles approximately building a strong basis for a lifestyles of abundance and safety.

Budgeting for Students and Young Adults
Chapter 10: Budgeting for Students and Young Adults

In the tumultuous journey of life, there's a specific segment that stands out as each thrilling and daunting - the transition from children to adulthood. As college students and young adults embark in this voyage, they're faced with a myriad of worrying situations, one of the most sizeable being the mastery of budgeting. In this monetary damage, we're capable of discover the monetary issues that scholars and young adults must be aware of, the stairs to construct a robust economic basis, and the pitfalls to keep away from in early financial manipulate.

Financial mistakes have the functionality to cast a protracted shadow over one's future. For students and young adults, some common pitfalls encompass excessive credit score card debt, a loss of monetary literacy leading to lousy finances picks and inadequate economic economic savings, neglecting the recognition quo of an emergency fund, and failing to cope with pupil loans and plan for the future. The gravity of these mistakes cannot be overstated, as they may avoid monetary stability and ward off development within the route of lengthy-time period goals.

To navigate the treacherous waters of pupil loans and credit score playing cards responsibly, humans have to exercising caution and prudence. It is essential to borrow handiest what's important, ensuring that the debt burden stays viable. Whether it's far scholar loans or credit score card debt, one need to hold in thoughts of the prolonged-time period implications of each economic choice. Swiping a credit score rating card may additionally offer instant gratification, however the outcomes can reverberate for destiny years. Therefore, it is important to pay credit score score card bills in whole every month, avoiding the lure of accumulating hobby and falling right into a debt spiral.

Building a robust economic basis for the future calls for a deliberate and strategic approach. The first step in this adventure is to get prepared. Students and young adults want to take stock in their contemporary-day financial situation, gaining a clean facts in their income, charges, and debt. This self-interest serves as a compass, guiding them in the direction of monetary stability and achievement.

Protecting oneself is each other important detail of building a robust financial basis. This includes establishing an emergency fund, a protection internet to cushion towards surprising conditions. By placing aside a element of their income regularly, university students and teenagers can create a monetary buffer that gives peace of thoughts and safeguards their economic well-being.

Prioritizing the reduction of excessive-hobby debt is a important step toward monetary freedom. By tackling debts with exorbitant hobby quotes, people can store themselves from being ensnared in a in no way-finishing cycle of payments. This strategic approach lets in them to regain manipulate over their fee variety and allocate belongings towards greater efficient endeavors.

Defining the most essential economic dreams is an important problem of building a strong economic foundation. Whether it is saving for a down fee on a house, starting a enterprise agency, or pursuing further schooling, having clean goals empowers college students and teenagers to make informed selections and allocate their assets accurately. These desires characteristic guiding stars, illuminating the course closer to economic prosperity.

Once the goals had been defined, it's time to put the plan into action. This entails developing a charge range that aligns with one's monetary goals and values. Budgeting gear and property can display worthwhile in this device. For students and teens, PocketGuard offers someone-nice platform to music spending and adhere to a finances. By recording transactions and monitoring improvement, people can live at the right song and make knowledgeable economic selections.

As with any journey, there are pitfalls to avoid along the way. Excessive and frivolous spending can erode even the maximum strong financial foundation. It is essential to exercising restraint and distinguish between wants and needs. Great fortunes are often out of place one dollar at a time, and with the aid of the use of the use of curbing needless fees, students and teenagers can hold their financial resources and pave the manner for a wealthy future.

Living on borrowed cash is any other perilous route to avoid. While credit score can provide short comfort, reliance on borrowed price range can result in a by no means-finishing cycle of debt. It is critical to stay inside one's way and keep away from the temptation of right now gratification on the charge of prolonged-time period economic stability.

Furthermore, it's miles critical to stand as plenty because the appeal of material possessions that may strain one's price range. Buying a brand new automobile or spending past one's method on a house can burden humans with excessive debt and limit their potential to preserve and invest for the future. By making prudent options and prioritizing monetary properly-being over right away gratification, college students and teenagers can guard their economic future.

Living paycheck to paycheck is a precarious situation that may perpetuate monetary lack of confidence. By failing to keep and make investments for the future, people go away themselves liable to surprising fees or monetary downturns. It is crucial to domesticate the dependancy of saving and allocate a element of every paycheck within the path of lengthy-time period financial goals.

Lastly, neglecting to spend money on retirement can also need to have an extended way-carrying out outcomes. Time is a precious asset, and via the usage of using starting early, college college students and teenagers can harness the power of compounding hobby to build a first rate retirement nest egg. By prioritizing retirement economic savings, they might make sure economic safety of their later years and enjoy the culmination in their tough work.

Budgeting for college students and teens is a vital expertise that lays the muse for a rich destiny. By keeping off commonplace monetary errors, navigating pupil loans and credit score score score gambling gambling cards responsibly, and building a robust economic basis, human beings can set themselves up for success. The adventure may be hard, however with willpower, concern, and the proper gear, college university college students and teens can hold close the paintings of budgeting and collect financial freedom. So, let us embark in this transformative adventure together, unlocking the secrets and techniques and techniques and techniques of financial prosperity and securing a colourful future.

Budgeting for Retirement and seniors

Chapter 17: Budgeting For Retirement And Seniors

Retirement is a monetary smash in lifestyles that many sit up for with excellent anticipation. It is a time of relaxation, exploration, and the pursuit of personal passions. However, a good way to fully revel in this stage of life, cautious budgeting and financial making plans are critical. In this financial ruin, we are able to delve into the factors that individuals want to maintain in thoughts at the same time as making plans for retirement, strategies for coping with healthcare and prolonged-time period care fees, advocated assets for retirement making plans and budgeting, and the suitable worrying conditions that seniors may additionally face in budgeting for their golden years.

Factors to Consider When Planning for Retirement: Retirement making plans is a complex tool that requires careful attention of various factors. Firstly, humans should decide their time horizons, thinking about their favored retirement age and existence expectancy. This will help them gauge how lengthy their retirement monetary savings want to last. Secondly, estimating costs is critical. It is essential to preserve in thoughts each critical charges, along with housing and healthcare, similarly to discretionary charges, which include tour and pastimes. Calculating required after-tax returns is each other essential step, as it allows human beings determine the charge of circulate returned they want on their investments to hold their favored life-style in retirement. Additionally, assessing danger tolerance is important, as it impacts the investment choices human beings make for their retirement economic savings. Lastly, property planning ought to not be neglected, because it guarantees that people' assets are allocated in keeping with their desires when they pass away. By considering the ones elements and beginning to devise for retirement as early as possible, humans can harness the power of compounding and set themselves up for economic safety in their golden years.

Ensuring Financial Security During Retirement: Financial safety all through retirement is a intention that many humans strive for. To acquire this, it's miles critical to take an honest stock of 1's belongings, monetary monetary savings, and investments. This inventory will offer a smooth image of 1's financial reputation and assist in placing practical desires for retirement. It is also essential to take into account personal alternatives and manner of existence selections at the same time as making plans for retirement. Factors together with desired sports activities activities, dwelling preparations, and proximity to loved ones need to be considered. Flexibility is key, as sudden modifications may also rise up in retirement. By having a plan this is adaptable to distinct times, individuals can navigate those changes simply and keep economic safety at some point of their retirement years.

Managing Healthcare and Long-Term Care Expenses: Healthcare and prolonged-time period care charges may be huge in the route of retirement. To manipulate the ones costs, people can do not forget severa strategies. One such technique is using a fitness economic savings account (HSA). An HSA is a unique financial financial savings account that can be contributed to till the age of sixty 5, even if no longer walking. It allows human beings to shop for healthcare fees on a tax-advantaged foundation. Traditional and Roth person retirement payments (IRAs) additionally may be done to buy healthcare charges in retirement. Additionally, having an emergency fund is essential to cowl surprising healthcare charges. Long-term care and incapacity earnings insurance are specific alternatives to don't forget, as they offer financial protection inside the occasion that long-term care is needed. By enforcing those strategies, humans can better manage their healthcare and prolonged-time period care charges, making sure a greater constant and fear-unfastened retirement.

Recommended Resources for Retirement Planning and Budgeting: When it entails retirement planning and budgeting, getting access to dependable sources and tools can considerably help human beings in making informed picks. Some encouraged assets include Fidelity, Betterment, Empower, Mint, Debt Calculators, and Vanguard. These structures provide a number of services, from retirement calculators to investment recommendation, to assist individuals plan and budget for his or her retirement effectively. By making use of those property, human beings can advantage valuable insights and make well-knowledgeable economic alternatives that align with their retirement desires.

Unique Challenges in Budgeting for Seniors: Budgeting for seniors provides its own set of specific annoying situations. One such challenge is the uncertainty of healthcare fees. As people age, healthcare charges will be inclined to boom, and it could be difficult to as it want to be are looking ahead to the ones costs. This uncertainty requires seniors to devise and price range for functionality healthcare costs, considering factors which incorporates inflation and the need for lengthy-time period care. Another undertaking is the functionality decline in earnings in some unspecified time inside the future of retirement. Many seniors depend on regular belongings of earnings, along with pensions and Social Security, which may not be enough to cover all prices. Seniors need to carefully charge range and prioritize their charges to make certain that their profits can maintain their desired lifestyle. Additionally, the emotional issue of transitioning into retirement can pose challenges. Seniors can also battle with the shortage in their professional identity and the adjustment to a extremely-modern routine. This emotional factor want to be considered while budgeting for retirement, as it can impact spending conduct and economic options. By acknowledging and addressing the ones particular annoying conditions, seniors can navigate their retirement years with greater ease and monetary stability.

Chapter 18: Automating Finances

In the quick-paced international we live in, time is of the essence. We locate ourselves continuously juggling more than one obligations, seeking to hold up with the desires of work, family, and personal life. In the midst of this chaos, handling our price variety can regularly end up a daunting project. But what if there has been a manner to streamline this way? A manner to automate our rate variety and loose up precious time and highbrow electricity? In this bankruptcy, we are able to discover the art of automating budget and the way it can supply peace of mind and financial stability.

Automating your bills is a essential step in simplifying your financial lifestyles. By installing automated invoice bills, you may ensure that your payments are paid on time, avoiding late fees and retaining a high-quality fee facts. This now not nice saves you cash however furthermore contributes to a healthful credit score score rating. Additionally, automating your payments allows you to spend a good deal much less time poring over spreadsheets and more time focusing at the matters that without a doubt depend variety.

One effective manner to installation computerized transfers and investments is thru direct deposit break up. By dividing your paycheck into special debts, you may allocate a part of your profits towards financial financial savings and investments with out even lifting a finger. Recurring financial monetary savings transfers are every other effective tool. By scheduling regular transfers out of your bank account to your monetary financial savings account, you can outcomes constructing up your economic financial savings through the years. Round-up monetary savings is a clever method wherein your purchases are rounded as a bargain because the closest dollar, and the distinction is robotically transferred in your economic savings account. This small change can upload as much as great financial savings in the long run. Goal-based absolutely transfers permit you to set particular monetary desires and routinely switch rate range towards conducting them. Lastly, making an funding spare exchange is a present day approach to making an funding, wherein small quantities of cash from your normal transactions are robotically invested in the inventory marketplace.

The blessings of automating your charge range go past sincerely saving time. It brings peace of mind and economic balance. By automating your invoice payments, you may make certain that they will be normally made on time, avoiding the stress and trouble of late charges. This moreover contributes to a super fee records, which performs a important characteristic in identifying your credit score score score rating. With automatic charge range, you not must constantly display your budgeting spreadsheet or fear about missing a rate. Instead, you can recognition on the larger picture and make monetary alternatives with self guarantee.

When it involves automating your finances, there are several device and assets to be had that will help you alongside the manner. FreshBooks, ERP, NetSuite, Xero, and QuickBooks are just a few examples of software program program application that would assist you in dealing with your price range correctly. These tool offer competencies along side bill pay, budgeting tools, and monitoring spending, making it a good deal much less hard than ever to live on top of your financial endeavor.

Security and reliability are paramount in terms of automating financial structures. Thankfully, improvements in generation have made it viable to ensure the safety of your economic data. AI, or synthetic intelligence, plays a large feature in financial services, providing advanced operations, reduced charges, advanced fraud detection, automatic regulatory compliance, and faster selection-making. By leveraging AI, monetary institutions can provide secure and reliable computerized structures that deliver people peace of mind.

Automating your fee variety is a pastime-changer in extremely-present day speedy-paced global. It allows you to streamline your bill bills, financial savings contributions, and investments, freeing up precious time and highbrow energy. With the proper device and property, you may automate your financial control and make certain the protection and reliability of your automated structures. So, why now not take the soar and grasp the art work of budgeting via automation? Your peace of mind and economic stability look beforehand to.

Incorporating Investments and Wealth Building Chapter 13: Incorporating Investments and Wealth Building

In the adventure inside the course of financial stability and prosperity, it is critical to not best interest on incomes and saving coins but additionally at the artwork of creating an funding and wealth constructing. This financial ruin delves into the strategies, concerns, and demanding situations associated with incorporating investments into your fee variety.

The first step inside the direction of constructing wealth is to make sure that you earn sufficient coins to cover your simple goals, with a few left over for saving. It is essential to have a strong foundation earlier than delving into the arena of investments. Once you have got got got installation a strong profits, the subsequent step is to govern your spending successfully, allowing you to maximize your economic financial savings. This requires subject, strength of mind, and a eager eye for distinguishing amongst want and desires.

Now comes the thrilling detail - making an funding your tough-earned cash in pretty some remarkable belongings. The key to a success making an funding lies in diversification. By spreading your investments during severa asset education, you lessen the chance related to any unmarried investment. This diversification guarantees that your portfolio is nicely-balanced and may weather the storms of the marketplace.

To collect proper diversification, it's far critical to recognition on preserving virtually one or fee range in each magnificence. By doing so, you can carefully don't forget how certainly one of a kind investments may additionally have interplay with every first rate. The purpose is to maintain uncorrelated assets, which skip in opposite suggestions, imparting the maximum diversification advantage. This way, if one funding plays poorly, the others may moreover compensate and preserve the overall balance of your portfolio.

Balancing danger and praise is a vital aspect of funding choice-making. Several elements need to be considered, together with your funding dreams, your normal mind-set in the direction of hazard, the investment time-frame, and the alternative belongings you keep. It is essential to assess your potential for loss and decide how a super deal hazard you're inclined to take on in pursuit of higher returns. Additionally, elements like credit score score threat and marketplace danger have to be cautiously evaluated to make informed investment selections.

Incorporating investments into your price variety requires careful making plans and consideration. Thankfully, there are numerous property and device to be had that will help you on this employer. When it entails budgeting software program, a number of the first-class options encompass QuickBooks, Xero, Zoho Books, PlanGuru, Float, and Centage Planning Maestro. These equipment will permit you to tune your income, prices, and investments, considering a complete overview of your economic scenario.

While the opportunity of creating an funding and constructing wealth is interesting, it's far essential to be aware of the functionality challenges and risks which might be available in conjunction with it. Economic situations, political instability, hobby costs, and geopolitical activities can all have an impact on market moves. Downturns within the marketplace can result in a decline within the charge of your investments, affecting both shares and bonds. It is vital to live knowledgeable, display your investments regularly, and be prepared to comply your approach at the same time as crucial.

Incorporating investments into your rate variety is a adventure that calls for endurance, data, and adaptability. By following the steps referred to in this financial disaster, you could begin to grasp the art of budgeting and take manage of your monetary future. Remember, building wealth is not an overnight technique, however with self-discipline and perseverance, you could pave the manner towards a rich and solid future.

Planning for Major Life Events

Chapter 19: Planning For Major Life Events

Life is complete of milestones and fundamental activities that form our journey. From weddings to seeking out a home, those moments aren't super super however furthermore require careful planning and budgeting. In this monetary disaster, we are able to explore the strategies and issues for budgeting for the ones most important existence occasions, making sure which you are well-prepared for the monetary transitions that consist of them.

The first step in making plans for critical existence occasions is to recognize your month-to-month income and costs. Understanding your economic scenario is crucial to create a practical finances. Take the time to assess your income sources and calculate your prices efficaciously. This will provide you with a clean photo of your economic popularity and help you are making informed picks.

Once you have got a clean records of your fee variety, it is time to begin budgeting for the correct occasion. For example, if you are making plans to buy a home, you need to finances on your down rate and thing in remaining prices. Determine how a bargain residence you could manage to pay for based totally on your economic situation and set a price range therefore. It's also vital to plan for home protection fees, as owning a domestic comes with additional prices past the preliminary buy.

When it includes weddings, setting priorities is top. Sit down collectively together along with your companion and speak what aspects of the wedding are most critical to you each. This will assist you allocate your finances for this reason and make certain which you are spending money at the matters that certainly rely to you. Create a price range that displays your priorities, and have in mind of your spending for the duration of the planning approach.

To hold your rate range organized and avoid any confusion, it is beneficial to keep your monetary economic financial savings separate for each important existence event. Open separate financial savings money owed for the marriage and your down price. This will no longer great assist you tune your development however moreover save you any unintended blending of charge variety. By preserving your economic financial savings separate, you could make sure which you are on path to satisfy your financial dreams for each event.

While making plans for primary lifestyles activities, it is essential to keep away from taking over new debt. Adding more economic responsibilities can positioned a pressure to your budget and make it tough to obtain your goals. Instead, reputation on handling your present debt and paintings toward paying it off. This will not excellent beautify your financial fitness but also provide you with more flexibility close to budgeting for crucial lifestyles sports.

In the face of sudden fees or monetary transitions, it is critical to have a plan in area. Stretching your price range and locating techniques to reduce prices will let you navigate the ones traumatic situations. Look for opportunities to barter fee plans for notable fees, permitting you to unfold out the monetary effect. If important, don't forget new borrowing alternatives, however be cautious and look at the terms and interest prices cautiously.

During instances of economic uncertainty, it may be tempting to liquidate investments. However, it's far crucial to exercising warning on the same time as making such picks. Consult with a financial advertising and advertising consultant earlier than liquidating any investments to ensure that you are making the fine preference on your prolonged-term monetary desires. Additionally, having emergency financial financial savings geared up for unexpected charges can offer you with a safety internet all through times of financial instability.

One of the right traumatic situations of budgeting for important life activities is the ability lack of earnings or task loss. To put together for this opportunity, it's miles essential to preserve a monetary monetary financial savings account. Determine your month-to-month charge variety and set aside a realistic amount to hold each month. By building up your financial savings, you can create a buffer to help you navigate any unexpected changes in your income.

In addition to the strategies stated above, there are numerous resources and equipment available to help you in budgeting for most essential existence activities. Google Sheets is a free spreadsheet that can be used to track your profits, fees, and economic savings. Mint is a complete cellphone app that offers a pinnacle level view of your rate variety and allows you positioned and music your price range. Goodbudget is a amateur-pleasant app that facilitates you allocate price variety to extremely good lessons and tune your spending. For shoppers, Personal Capital offers a unfastened cellular telephone app that allows you to govern your investments and track your net well worth. Lastly, GnuCash is a loose computer software application especially designed for small corporation owners to control their rate variety correctly.

As you embark on the journey of budgeting for maximum critical existence activities, it's far critical to be aware of the capacity traumatic situations and concerns that might upward thrust up. These demanding situations embody a loss of income or hobby loss, sudden costs, immoderate debt, the need for financial independence, overspending, horrible credit score, and a loss of financial financial savings. By acknowledging these capability hurdles, you may take proactive steps to mitigate their impact on your financial nicely-being.

Chapter 20: Dealing With Financial Setbacks

In lifestyles, we frequently face unexpected traumatic conditions that could throw our economic balance off balance. These setbacks can are available various office works, which embody interest loss, scientific emergencies, or surprising expenses. When faced with such situations, it's miles crucial to have the resilience and backbone to conquer them. In this chapter, we're able to discover strategies to help you navigate through monetary setbacks and emerge more potent than ever.

The first step in dealing with any economic setback is to evaluate your present day situation. Take a 2d to reflect at the quantity of the setback and understand its effect in your normal financial well-being. This self-popularity will assist you benefit readability and develop a course of action.

Once you have got assessed your situation, it is time to prioritize your costs. Determine which expenses are critical and which may be in short reduced or removed. By decreasing again on non-crucial fees, you may loose up charge variety to deal with greater urgent economic obligations.

In instances of financial worry, it's far critical to talk collectively together with your lenders and lenders. Reach out to them and deliver an cause of your state of affairs in reality. Many monetary institutions provide assistance packages or bendy fee alternatives for people going through economic setbacks. By proactively engaging collectively together with your lenders, you may be able to negotiate extra manageable fee phrases.

Exploring extra belongings of profits also can assist alleviate monetary stress. Consider taking over a factor-time interest or freelancing opportunities to complement your modern-day-day income. Every little bit lets in, and these greater earnings can circulate an extended manner in helping you regain your monetary balance.

Seeking professional assistance is another important step in overcoming financial setbacks. Financial therapists are knowledgeable to provide guidance and manual in navigating via monetary demanding conditions. They can educate you on sound financial behavior, help you triumph over debt, and provide the plenty-needed social assist throughout this hard time. Don't hesitate to achieve out to a professional who can guide you thru the manner of rebuilding your monetary lifestyles.

Now that we have noted various techniques to triumph over monetary setbacks, permit's discover the adventure of human beings who have efficiently recovered from such stressful situations. These achievement reminiscences characteristic a testomony to the truth that with energy of mind and the right approach, it is possible to get higher from even the most hard monetary situations.

One such success tale is that of Sarah, who positioned herself drowning in debt after a sequence of unfortunate sports. Sarah took the first step by way of the use of using identifying the trouble and acknowledging the want for trade. She then created a rate variety to advantage manipulate over her price variety and prioritize her charges. By cutting back on useless charges and paying in coins, Sarah became able to regularly lessen her debt.

Sarah also made a conscious try and keep away from taking up any new debt. She resisted the temptation to shop for new topics and centered on residing within her method. Additionally, she sought guidance from a economic consultant who helped her broaden an prolonged-time period economic plan. With perseverance and issue, Sarah turn out to be able to boom her income via diverse thing hustles, which in addition prolonged her journey in the direction of financial restoration.

While handling economic setbacks, it's miles critical to cope with the emotional worrying situations that would rise up. It is not uncommon to experience emotions of melancholy, tension, disgrace, and embarrassment. These feelings ought to have a profound impact on our ordinary properly-being and prevent our improvement toward monetary recuperation.

To fight the ones emotional demanding situations, it's far vital to prioritize self-care. Engage in activities that bring you satisfaction and offer a revel in of remedy. Surround yourself with a manual gadget this is aware and empathizes at the side of your situation. By looking for solace inside the organisation of cherished ones, you may discover the energy to triumph over the emotional hurdles that come with economic setbacks.

Chapter 21: Maintaining A Sustainable Budget

In the journey of gaining knowledge of the art of budgeting, it is not sufficient to create a rate variety and hold on with it. Life is ever-converting, and as such, our goals and goals evolve over time. Therefore, it's far critical to often compare and alter our price range to make sure its sustainability and alignment with our financial aspirations.

Why is it important to check and adjust the price range often? The answer lies inside the reality that our lives are in ordinary motion. Our needs and dreams exchange as we increase and evolve. By reviewing our fee variety month-to-month and yearly, we gain precious insights into our spending conduct and economic styles. This introspection permits us to recognize the way to revise our price range to higher meet our present day and destiny financial desires.

Staying stimulated and committed to our monetary goals may be a task, however it is important for keeping a sustainable finances. To benefit this, we must first apprehend the reason at the back of our monetary dreams. Understanding why we are pursuing those goals offers us the electricity and backbone to live on track. Additionally, putting S.M.A.R.T. (Specific, Measurable, Achievable, Relevant, Time-positive) dreams allows us break down our prolonged-term aspirations into smaller, extra practicable steps.

Breaking our long-time period goals into smaller saving desires is every other effective method for staying inspired. By reaching those smaller milestones along the way, we are able to have a laugh our improvement and hold our enthusiasm for the budgeting adventure. Keeping a monetary mag and monitoring our development lets in us to visually see how a ways we've got come, reinforcing our strength of mind to our desires. Surrounding ourselves with like-minded people who share our economic aspirations also can provide manual and encouragement while the going receives hard.

Lastly, making our dreams seen, whether or not or now not thru imaginative and prescient forums or reminders, maintains them at the forefront of our minds, serving as a regular reminder of why we're budgeting inside the first region.

Celebrating milestones and successes alongside our budgeting journey is essential for retaining motivation and a powerful mind-set. Every little success, regardless of how small, deserves reputation. When paying off debt, for example, it's far important to have a laugh the ones victories. Rewarding ourselves with some factor we rate, whether or not or not it's far our favorite dessert or a cutting-edge-day clothing item, reinforces the notion that success isn't pretty lots the stop forestall result however is likewise part of the journey we are project. By celebrating these milestones, we create a terrific affiliation with budgeting, making it more likely that we will maintain in this direction.

Maintaining a sustainable budget calls for more than surely energy of thoughts and resolution. It additionally includes using belongings and equipment that could assist us in our economic adventure. There are numerous encouraged belongings and strategies that could help us stay on route. Buying clothing secondhand, for example, no longer great saves coins however furthermore promotes sustainability. Using what we already have earlier than shopping for new items is each unique manner to lessen pointless costs. Trying samples before splurging on outstanding splendor products allows us make informed looking for selections. Additionally, adopting a DIY mind-set with regards to responsibilities throughout the residence can keep cash on hiring specialists. Outsmarting the grocery store through growing a buying list and sticking to it, similarly to developing our very own meals from scraps, are effective approaches to reduce grocery costs. Lastly, it's far critical no longer to install writing off chain shops, as they regularly provide low cost options for various desires.

Despite our high-quality efforts, there may be challenges and boundaries that we encounter even as maintaining a charge variety. It is vital to be privy to those capacity roadblocks and function techniques in vicinity to conquer them. Spending too much on housing can strain our finances, so it's far critical to find out a balance that aligns with our monetary desires. A lack of a described finances also can keep away from our development, because it leaves room for overspending and financial uncertainty. The mind-set of "I'll hold once I make extra money" may be destructive to our financial well-being, because it perpetuates the cycle of residing past our way. Setting a measurable economic savings reason offers a clean goal to artwork in the path of, keeping us stimulated and responsible. Student loan payments also can be a awesome impediment, but by way of the usage of incorporating them into our charge range and searching for compensation alternatives, we will manage them correctly. Lastly, it's far crucial to keep in thoughts of our comfort sector and keep away from overusing credit score rating gambling cards, as they can result in debt and financial instability.

Maintaining a sustainable rate range calls for self-control, adaptability, and the willingness to adjust our economic plans as our lives change. By frequently reviewing and adjusting our rate range, staying brought on and celebrating milestones, utilising encouraged belongings, and overcoming ability demanding conditions, we're able to hold close the art work of budgeting and acquire our monetary dreams. Remember, the journey in the route of economic freedom is not easy, however with perseverance and a well-maintained rate range, it's miles inside our reach.

Embracing a Financially Empowered Future
Chapter 17: Embracing a Financially Empowered Future

As we near the give up of our adventure within the path of gaining knowledge of the art work of budgeting, it is essential to reflect at the personal growth and financial achievements we've got made along the way. These achievements can take many paperwork, each tangible and intangible. From attaining a financial purpose or winning an award to studying a cutting-edge potential or improving a courting, each accomplishment is a testomony to our electricity of mind and perseverance.

But how can we ensure that our dedication to budgeting and financial manipulate maintains into the destiny? The solution lies in making conscious selections, making an investment in ourselves, and planning our spending accurately. By selecting carefully wherein we allocate our resources, we are capable of prioritize our monetary well-being and set ourselves up for extended-time period fulfillment.

Investing in ourselves is going beyond in reality economic investments. It approach making an investment in our records, abilities, and personal increase. By constantly reading and increasing our horizons, we're able to adapt to the ever-changing economic landscape and make knowledgeable choices. Whether it is through taking publications, attending workshops, or looking for mentorship, making an investment in ourselves is a crucial step towards monetary empowerment.

Planning our spending is a few different key component of preserving our financial journey. By developing a finances and sticking to it, we're capable of make certain that our cash is allotted correctly and in alignment with our goals. Saving turns into a addiction, and we find out ourselves more resilient in the face of sudden prices. Learning to make investments accurately is also essential, as it lets in us to increase our wealth and regular our financial destiny.